diningspaces

TEXT
kathleen antonson

PHOTOGRAPHY
david matheson

STYLING
nadine bush

EXECUTIVE EDITOR
clay ide

BONNIER
BOOKS

 BONNIER
BOOKS

This edition published by Bonnier Books,
Appledram Barns, Birdham Road, Chichester,
West Sussex PO20 7EQ, UK

WELDON OWEN

Chief Executive Officer John Owen
President & Chief Operating Officer Terry Newell
Chief Financial Officer Christine E. Munson
Vice President, Publisher Roger Shaw
Vice President, Creative Director Gaye Allen
Vice President, International Sales Stuart Laurence

Associate Publisher Shawna Mullen
Senior Art Director Emma Boys
Managing Editor Sarah Lynch
Production Director Chris Hemesath
Colour Manager Teri Bell
Photo Co-ordinator Elizabeth Lazich
UK Translation Grant Laing Partnership

Set in Simoncini Garamond™ and Formata™

Colour separations by International Color Services
Printed in Singapore by Tien Wah Press (Pte.) Ltd.

Originally printed as *Pottery Barn Dining Spaces* in 2004.
10 9 8 7 6 5 4 3 2 1

ISBN: 978-1-905825-05-9

A Place to Celebrate

Good food and good company are two of life's greatest pleasures, and the dining room is where these pleasures come together. From breakfast nooks to patios, today's dining spaces extend throughout the home; whether indoors or out, they can set the stage for holidays, birthdays, and special occasions with versatility, style, and warmth.

The best dining areas welcome the varied scope of life's events: everyday meals, family games, and Christmas toasts should all be equally served by the space. We wrote this book to show you how well-chosen furniture, smart lighting, and accessible storage all help to make dining at home an experience to enjoy and remember.

We promote the blend of tradition and personality that is the hallmark of contemporary dining. Our approach is to provide a wealth of options so you can meet the challenges of your own unique space. We photographed this book in real homes, and filled it with easy ways to apply what you see to your own dining space. The information presented here can be readily adapted to rooms of all shapes and sizes. In *Dining Spaces*, you'll find ideas and inspiration for a place that brings friends and family together, and makes all who enter feel right at home.

contents

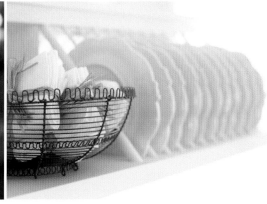

your style

The dining room, whether it's part of a kitchen or a separate space all its own, holds a central place in our most cherished notions about home. This is the place where families gather to share good food, good company, and laughter. Welcoming friends and relatives to the dining room table is the natural way to celebrate special holidays, but it can also make even the simplest meal a special event.

Great dining rooms may differ vastly in form, but they all share a focus on warmth and welcome that inspires their designs. Success lies work surface for crafts; a set-up on a porch that's a perfect place for cocktails; a low table that can double as a coffee table drawn up to a hearth.

Even the most formal dining room can be used every day. Making it a place for work, hobbies, or family board games can add character and warmth to the room. Balance the refined with the casual to get more use out of the dining room: layering an heirloom mahogany table with simple tea-towel place mats or replacing formal chairs with a bench makes the room as suited to casual suppers as it is to festive banquets.

The perfect dining room shifts easily from a place for entertaining to a serene space for relaxing. Start with great basics and your dining room will adapt to any occasion.

in keeping the comfort of both you and your guests in mind as you decorate the room. Start with quality basic furnishings that balance looks and comfort: a traditional table and chairs, plus storage pieces for everyday convenience. Add an elegant rug, a stylish chandelier, and table-top accessories to customize the space.

A dining room can be as simple as a small table and two chairs arranged in a cosy corner or as grand as a long banquet table in a large, separate room. Whatever space you have, most dining areas serve as more than just a place to eat and entertain. Choose furnishings with flexibility in mind: a rustic table that also makes a convenient

The standard dining room arrangement – a table surrounded by chairs – is inspired as much by necessity as it is by tradition. As a result, dining spaces are not redecorated as often as other rooms. Compensate for that permanence with small embellishments. Reinvent the whole room with seasonal decorations, loose covers for chairs, or a quick change of linen. For a more dramatic make-over, paint a single wall in a vivid colour.

Like the meals served in it, a dining area's decor is best when it's imaginative and artfully presented. Select a classic table, comfortable chairs, and soft lighting. Add inspired details, and every meal will be a feast worth sharing.

Easy Elegance for Everyday Dining

A classic dining room is like the perfect little black dress. You can count on it for almost any occasion. Start with basics that create simple elegance. Change the accents to dress the room up or down or take it from day to night. Well-chosen details turn a tasteful space into a place to celebrate.

The best dining rooms are not only comfortable and beautiful, but also adaptable. They're a welcoming place for family suppers, formal dinner parties, and every type of special gathering in between. They begin with a spacious table that works well for a variety of tasks, including dining and working. When choosing a table, consider its stability as well as its shape and size. To ensure comfortable seating and enough space to accommodate large parties, allow at least 60 cm (2 ft) per person around the table.

A good place to start when selecting dining room furniture is a classic set-up for eight: a rectangular table surrounded by eight chairs. You can alter this arrangement according to the size of your space or the number of guests you regularly entertain. A 2 m (6 ft) table seats six to eight, a 1.2 m (4 ft) round table seats up to six, and a 90 cm (3 ft) square table is perfect for four or for an intimate dinner for two.

Simplicity is the essence of style. Once you've chosen a table, add crisp white linen and streamlined china that's suitable for formal and casual dining alike. Use a neutral colour palette and your room can shift gears effortlessly. Set out sparkling stemware and candles for a special occasion, or use a colourful runner for more relaxed gatherings.

Glass cheese domes, *left*, capture the beauty of white tuberoses and tulips. **Linen table runners**, *right*, add polish without being as formal as a full tablecloth. Laid across the width of the table, they frame each place setting.

In this striking dining room, a simple table is laid with a light touch for a wine and cheese tasting. For a casual event such as this – more than a buffet but short of a four-course meal – use hem-stitched linen runners in place of a tablecloth and paper tags as informal place cards. A large centrepiece composed of one type of flower gives a sense of abundance to the table. (Flowers with little or no scent, such as tulips, won't interfere with the aromas of the meal.) Platters placed at either end of the table make passing dishes easier and more convenient. Encourage guests to mingle by setting food and drinks out at various stations throughout the room, and introduce different cheese and wine pairings at each station.

A classic dining room, *left*, is often based on symmetry, with a centrepiece in the middle of the table and rows of matching chairs. **A paper place card**, *above*, lashed with lengths of colourful raffia, adds casual style to white linen.

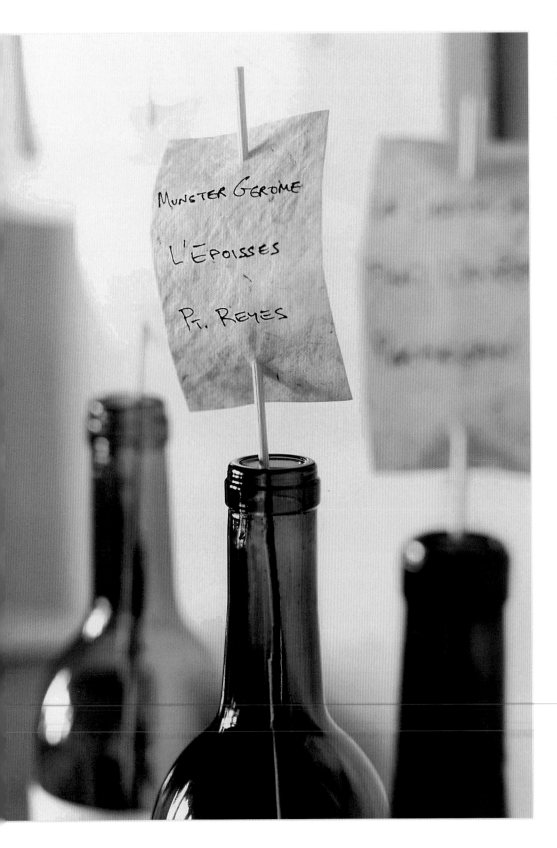

This wine and cheese party is a casual affair, but subtle elegance is conveyed through the details. Several cheese selections are set out on sturdy cutting boards with knives and slicers nearby for easy self-service; strategically placed on a sideboard, their pungent aromas won't interfere with tasting at the table. To clear the palate between bites, slices of plain bread are provided in ample supply. Shapely decanters are filled to the widest part of the vessel to allow the red wine to breathe before tasting.

Entertaining your guests in style is easy: it's all in the thoughtful details.

Guests can confidently pair cheeses and wines with the help of simple menus. Bamboo skewers in wine bottles display cards with suggested cheese pairings. Paper leaves line the cutting boards to add a bit of seasonal colour and texture to the serene palette of the room. A wine collection can be stored in the open to make an elegant display, with each bottle wrapped in tissue, secured with a paper sticker.

A cheese menu, *left*, is displayed in a decanted bottle of the wine that best suits the selections. **A modular mahogany wine bar**, *right*, becomes a culinary still life, with bottles wrapped in tissue paper – white wine in white, red wine in natural.

Design Details

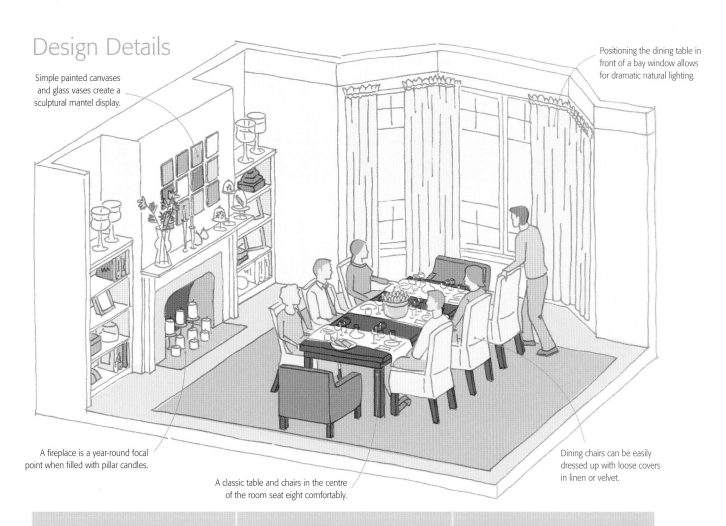

Simple painted canvases and glass vases create a sculptural mantel display.

Positioning the dining table in front of a bay window allows for dramatic natural lighting.

A fireplace is a year-round focal point when filled with pillar candles.

A classic table and chairs in the centre of the room seat eight comfortably.

Dining chairs can be easily dressed up with loose covers in linen or velvet.

Colour Palette

If you like the simplicity of white but still want some colour, consider neutrals, usually variations of white, beige, or grey. These muted hues are calming and restful. They blend well with each other and combine nicely with other colours such as the soft yellow on the walls in this dining room. They also work well as a backdrop to accessories, whether you add a colourful accent with linen or change the mood with flowers.

Room Plan

There's a reason the traditional dining room arrangement has endured: it works. If you're lucky enough to have a room with good proportions, setting it up is easy. Simply placing the table front and centre can give any dining space a classic atmosphere. In this dining room, a long banquet table and a set of chairs with high, straight backs give the room presence. To create this effect, choose furniture with oversize, comfortable proportions, which will place focus on the centre of the room. Loose covers add flexibility for seasonal style.

Materials

Hem-stitch linen A classic for dining, linen is decorative and durable. Finished with an intricate needlework border, hem-stitch linen adds elegance to any table.

Glass A sparkling addition to any table, smooth glass has less surface area than cut glass, which offers many facets for reflecting light.

Leather Luxurious and supple, leather softens with age and use. In some cases, leather will change colour slightly over time.

Bistro Breakfast

Your favourite corner bistro lets you linger with friends or daydream in delicious solitude. With a few comfortable furnishings you can re-create that atmosphere in your own kitchen.

Make a breakfast nook or a little-used corner of the kitchen cheerful and irresistible with a small round table and a few chairs. Adopt the style of continental bistros and stack coffee cups and breakfast wares close by or directly on the table. Try tucking a table under or alongside a window with a view to make the seating area feel larger. When space is at a premium, an étagère with selections of jam, coffee, and tea transforms breakfast into a special event.

Classic bentwood chairs, *opposite*, reflect continental bistro style and make the space feel more airy. **On a small table**, *left*, an étagère conserves space and offers everything needed for a casual breakfast. Used as a caddy, it's easy to whisk away to restock or to clear the table. **A handsome stainless steel espresso maker**, *above*, paired with plenty of cups makes an attractive and practical display, arranged within arm's reach of the table.

How to Design a Place Setting

As soon as you were old enough to lay the table, you learned to place a folded napkin to the left of the plate and then set a fork on top of it. The knife and spoon were easy; they belonged on the other side of the plate. Glasses were arranged over the knife and spoon, and plates were stacked according to course. You'll never go wrong with this classic place setting, but when the celebration or the mood calls for something more imaginative, it's okay to bend the rules in the spirit of creativity.

Numbered napkins, *opposite*, let guests know where they are in a four-course meal. A stack of smooth river rocks is glued together to serve as a place card. Ample square trays replace chargers, to handsome effect. **A slim leather bracelet**, *above left*, has a dual role – it secures the napkin and is a lovely party favour for guests. A simple strip of kraft paper guides guests to their seats, where sparkling blue glasses punctuate the neutral table. **A witty pocketed place mat**, *below left*, leaves no question as to where the cutlery goes; a miniature easel does the same for guests, directing them to their seats.

entertaining

For the host, the fun of entertaining begins long before the guests begin to arrive. Take pleasure in creating a dynamic guest list and assembling a tempting menu. Then, decide which kind of dining style best suits the event. Does the occasion call for a sit-down dinner? Or would you like to encourage conversation with a lively cocktail hour and a family-style meal? To create a truly casual atmosphere, serve the meal buffet-style or simply set out hors d'oeuvres.

Once you know the number of guests, take stock of your dining surfaces and floor space.

If you're entertaining a large group, think about setting up a temporary dining area in the living room or even in a generously sized hallway. It can be fun to decorate a new space for the occasion. For an intimate gathering, you might try placing a small table by a fireplace or near a wall of windows with a spectacular view.

You already know that lighting influences the mood of a party almost as much as the choice of music and decorations. To get the light level just right for the event, you may need to add or subtract a few table lamps. Candles provide the ulti-

Hosting a memorable gathering should be as enjoyable as attending the event. Take pleasure in planning a menu, then add the little details that make the mood festive.

If you have a long table surrounded by lots of chairs, but you imagine a casual, eat-as-you-please party, pull the chairs away from the table and use the surface as a single, long sideboard. Table too small to accommodate twelve for a sit-down meal? Add to the existing layout by gathering occasional tables from elsewhere in the house and covering them with matching table-cloths. Encourage mingling by arranging informal areas for conversation with convenient places to set drinks and small plates. When setting up the space, be aware of potential bottlenecks, especially near food and drinks, and be sure to leave enough room for guests to move freely.

mate party glow, but don't use them as the only light source or else the room may be too dark.

After you've addressed the essentials – a dining style, furniture arrangement, and lighting – it's time to consider the essential details. Basic party planning strategies, such as making a log of the guest list, menu, and seating arrangement, can help keep things running smoothly. Gestures as simple as a handwritten place card or flowers tucked in each napkin make memorable favours and show your guests how much you care. In the end, however, the most important part of entertaining is making your guests feel welcome, and enjoying the time you spend together.

Creating a Banquet

Delicious food, close friends, and beautiful surroundings are essential to a celebration, but it's the unexpected details that give a party its own special style. Once you've assembled the basics, add imaginative place settings and clever accessories to make it an occasion to remember.

Party hats and trumpets may have gone the way of childhood, but any banquet can be exuberant and energetic just the same. Set the mood with a playful approach that extends to the details. Greet guests with decorations and favours placed at every level, from the top of the mantel to the backs of the chairs. From the moment company arrives, fête them with charming mementos – some elegant, some handmade – that pay tribute to the evening and the occasion.

There are lots of ways to set up a banquet, each lending itself to a different kind of decoration. A group of separate small tables evokes the lighthearted atmosphere of a bistro. Lining up tables end to end in one long unit is convivial but also more formal. If you choose a long table, create a sweet, friendly tableau by draping it in flowing linen. You'll need extra seating, and although borrowed or rented chairs are fine, alternating your everyday dining chairs with gold-painted flea-market finds creates a charming mix-and-match look. Personalized decorations at each place setting – an artistically rendered menu or tissue-lined paper bags filled with favours – create a presentation that looks great as a whole and makes every guest feel special.

A gleaming Murano glass cherry, *left*, greets each guest as they arrive at the table and draws their attention to the menu. **Clever gift bags**, *right*, are made by lining brown paper lunch bags with tissue and tying one to the back of each chair with a length of voile ribbon.

Since the banquet table itself already suggests a special occasion, it's fun to style it with some wit instead of using formal, traditional decorations. At this birthday party, shimmery lamps stand sentry down the middle of the table, replacing the expected candlesticks or floral arrangements. Beaded lampshades give an especially pretty tinted downlight day or night, and lamp flexes can be cleverly hidden by running them under the tablecloth and between the tables. Fragrant flowers are strewn about in place of gathered bouquets, lightly scenting the table and reinforcing a leisurely and playful atmosphere.

Metres of pressed linen, *left*, cover this table. Fashioned from a continuous bolt, the cloth covers four small square tables, creating the illusion of a single long banquet table. **Small bottles of champagne**, *above*, are individually chilled in their own "ice buckets", and each is served with a charming straw.

Creative place settings can establish a theme for celebrations large and small. A neutral-toned tablecloth and coloured linen napkins radiate style without the dressed-up air of plain white. Polaroid place cards, snapped as each guest arrives, add an enticing personal touch. The host might collect them after dinner to give to the guest of honour or send each one home individually as a favour.

A unique banquet table invites lingering with a clever mix of humour and casual sophistication.

Menu cards placed on top of each napkin immediately engage guests, beckoning them to peruse the courses of the meal to come – a nice touch for banquet-style parties at which guests may not know the people sitting around them. Food is an interesting topic to almost anyone, and a compelling menu is a good way to start a conversation. Menus can be handwritten, designed on a home computer, or professionally printed at a local printing shop.

Portrait place cards, *left*, are snapshots taken as each guest arrives, and their placement directs each guest to the right seat at the table. **Beaded lampshades**, *right*, glimmer any time of day and cast a warm, flattering glow at night. Polished metal lamp bases further reflect the light.

Serving dessert in the living area is a way to keep a banquet mood casual. People are free to move around and serve themselves after the main meal, while the confections and pretty coffee cups embellish the space. Instead of serving one large cake, arrange cupcakes, piled high with icing, on a cake stand as an inviting alternative that also makes it easy for guests to help themselves.

When entertaining, presentation is everything. A low coffee table – either covered with a festive runner or left unadorned – makes the perfect staging ground for an informal yet convivial after-dinner coffee service.

Garlands of white carnations, *left*, hang in various lengths from a bamboo rod over the fireplace. **Cupcakes presented on a scalloped cake stand**, *above*, are served on fine china. **Birthday gifts**, *right*, adorn a festive mantel in full view of guests as they enjoy dessert.

Design Details

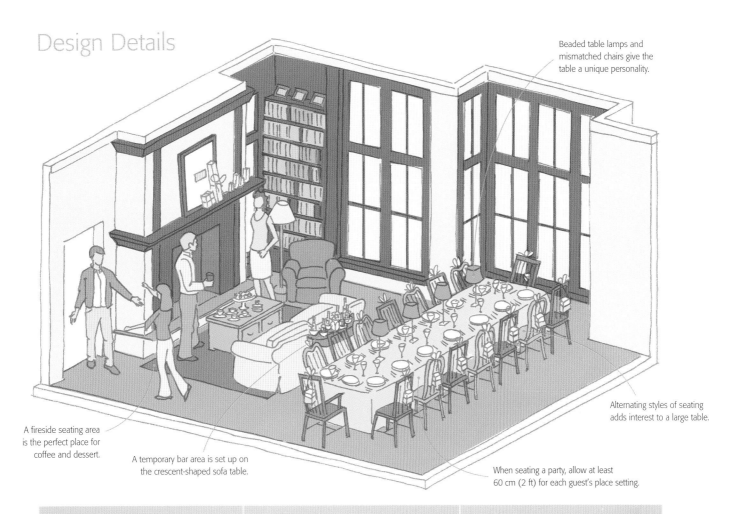

Beaded table lamps and mismatched chairs give the table a unique personality.

A fireside seating area is the perfect place for coffee and dessert.

A temporary bar area is set up on the crescent-shaped sofa table.

Alternating styles of seating adds interest to a large table.

When seating a party, allow at least 60 cm (2 ft) for each guest's place setting.

Colour Palette

Attractive wood panelling and wood floors create the foundation for the warm colour palette in this room. Pale amber walls add a light note to the layered cinnamon and chocolate shades of the woodwork and furniture. The table is dressed to reflect the colour palette as well, with coppery beaded lampshades and table linen in a rich shade of mocha. White candles, flowers, and china become bright accents in the room.

Room Plan

A generous banquet table, fashioned from several square tables lined up, spans the width of this room without crowding it. Because the table is narrow, this set-up takes up less space than you might think. By rearranging other furniture around the fireplace, every piece in the room is put to work to serve the party. The mantel becomes a shelf for gifts, the coffee table is a second gathering place laid out festively for dessert. A crescent-shaped table becomes the bar with a charming offering of small bottles of champagne set out for guests to help themselves.

Materials

Redwood Beautiful and durable, redwood is used for both interiors and exteriors. Indoors, it's typically used to frame windows and enhance strong architectural lines.

Beading An elegant alternative to solid fabric accessories, beaded lampshades and accent pieces shimmer as they reflect light.

White oak Featuring a pronounced intricate grain, white oak floors are desirable for their ability to absorb vibration and sound.

How to Add the Finishing Touch

Laying the table is one of the enjoyable rituals of entertaining. But often it's the inspired finishing touch – the fold of a napkin, an amusing place card, a clever napkin ring – that provides the real fun. You may even be tempted to put out these accessories first and then design the table top around them. Give creativity free rein and brighten each place setting with a witty flourish. Ideas are just as likely to be found at the greengrocer's or jeweller's or in a toy shop as they are in the china cupboard. Exult in the irreverent; fasten napkins with vintage jewellery, prop place cards with fruit or vegetables, or let a toy lorry hold a few flowers.

Clever details set the mood, *above*. The table is ideal for presenting guests with a small blossom tucked in a napkin, pretty cord or ribbon tied around cutlery, or a place card fashioned from a simple tag, like the one shown here. **Rules are things of the past**, *right*, when it comes to place settings. During the Victorian era, white linen and a fleet of silver had to be set in proper order by each plate. Now, colourful napkins can be tucked in the glass, set between soup bowl and plate, or bound in all manner of clever napkin rings, such as an antique star-shaped biscuit cutter.

Place card inspirations, *left*, can be found almost anywhere. Here, toy blackboards stand in, but garden stakes, smooth stones, or seashells would do just as well (and all can be personalized with ink or paint). **Don't eat your vegetables**, *below left*, if you can use them to make a place setting look great. Here, a portobello mushroom sets the tone for fresh, simple fare to come. **Inventive napkin folding**, *above*, makes it easy to create new looks for every occasion. Simply roll napkins and neatly secure them with a bracelet or ribbon. You can also create an informal look by knotting napkins in the centre. Try out the casual triangle fold, the fan, or the starched "Bishop's mitre".

space

Imagine a dining room that's as comfortable as a living room – a room that's always in use and invites lingering over delicious meals and lively conversation. A clever space plan can help coax this dream into reality. To design your ideal dining room, keep company in mind, but focus on family. Sharing food is by nature a close, familial affair, and a dining room should convey that sense of intimacy, no matter what its size.

To create the room you want, you must first realistically assess the one you have. Is the kitchen table or one end of the great room the "real" dining room in your house? In places where your family congregates, you can either give in and make a dining room of the area you use most frequently, or find ways to direct your family into a separate space. If you choose the latter, you may invite more use of a dining room simply by redecorating in a basic style that can dress up for entertaining, rather than down for everyday use. Examine the room as a whole – not just as a home for tables and chairs, but as a gathering place – to help you plan your layout. To scale down a large room, you might create a few places for eating and others for conversation instead of focussing on one central dining area. Or, replace chairs with benches at the table for a sense of camaraderie. In small spaces, tables that expand allow practical pursuits as well as dining. Make the most of the floor plan with a drop-leaf style or a table which extends to seat extra guests or which expands to accommodate work and craft projects.

No dining space should feel too small. Luckily, it's often the way a room is organized, and not its size, that makes it feel crowded. If your dining room is a hub of activity, space planning that smooths traffic flow will help make it a more pleasant place to be. Determine how you move from this space to other rooms in the house and arrange your furnishings accordingly, even if it means removing some pieces altogether.

An open plan looks uncluttered and has the added benefit of allowing space for activities other than dining. Setting the table off to one side or in an alcove creates an intimate room within a room. Before you start moving furniture, sketch out your ideas on paper. Make a scale floor plan with movable paper cut-outs of all your furniture pieces. Once you have a plan that feels logical, try it out with your real furnishings, but remain flexible. There's no substitute for day-to-day use to determine if a layout suits your needs.

A smart dining room layout is user-friendly. Plan a space that creates a sense of welcome and makes guests and family feel special, no matter what the occasion.

Hosting a Casual Buffet

Buffet-style dining is one of the easiest ways to entertain a crowd. Set out the food to tempt guests to nibble, and arrange furniture to encourage mingling. Provide plenty of seats for eating and socializing, with space for plates and drinks nearby. Make the space as inviting as the menu.

The "great room" once served as the centre of the household – a single space in which to cook, eat, and entertain. Many of today's open-plan home designs continue to reflect that early gathering spirit. There's still no better way to enjoy time with family and friends than to bring delicious food into the equation. A buffet approach to dining puts the focus on time spent together and makes entertaining casual, easy, and fun.

If you have an open-plan space, the room's arrangement can help with the hard work of hosting. Make guests comfortable by placing generous armchairs and a sofa close to a fireplace. Provide enough seating for everyone by setting small groups of benches and chairs throughout the room to inspire conversation and shared laughter.

Arrange the serving table to continue the easy-going mood. Make sure there's enough space around the buffet and decorate the table simply to allow guests plenty of room to manoeuvre. Pressed linen, gathered wildflowers, and cutlery bundled in napkins work equally well for gatherings great and small. Plates and condiments set on both sides of a long table help guests navigate along the buffet.

A traditional buffet, *left*, is set for a casual meal to be enjoyed in the seating area in front of the fireplace. The curly redwood of the mantel is found in other architectural details such as the door frames. **Blades of grass**, *right*, decorate easy-to-carry bundles of napkins and cutlery.

Arrange plates at one end of the table and cutlery at the other for smooth traffic flow at the buffet.

Where space allows, a buffet table that's pulled away from the wall lets guests help themselves to food from both sides. A two-line buffet serves a large group quickly and efficiently. By arranging dishes at one end, serving pieces in the middle, and cutlery on the other, you can suggest a traffic pattern that guides guests to pick up their plates, move along the table with hands free to serve themselves, and take up their cutlery last. Place drinks in another part of the room to avoid traffic jams at the food table. If there's only space for a small table, distribute some of the buffet around the room: appetizers on a sideboard, salad and bread on a console table, desserts on a coffee table. Set out easily spilled foods, such as soups and main courses served *au jus*, last in the buffet line, making them easier to carry and closer to the seating.

A wall of windows framed in redwood reveals a lush vista. The room's everyday dining table is pushed up against the windows, allowing guests extra space to move along the temporary buffet. It also provides an extra surface for serving dishes and acts as a drop-off space for cocktail glasses.

The mark of a good buffet dinner party is how easily guests can help themselves to whatever they want to eat and drink. It's helpful to create a second, separate area for beverages to keep people circulating around the room. Clear a shelf or desk and put it to use as a self-service bar so that guests won't have to juggle food plates and drinks at the same time.

Set out a portable bar and snacks on a deep shelf to encourage guests to help themselves.

To keep the visual clutter of a well-stocked bar from overpowering a dining room, choose one with concealed storage or create a portable bar that can be put away when not in use. One way to do this elegantly is to fill a sturdy, handled, flat-bottomed basket with liquor and liqueurs and arrange the bottles in descending height back-to-front so that the offerings are easily visible. Set out enough glasses in appropriate sizes for different drinks, and incorporate artwork or still-life displays to make the bar area an interesting focal point.

Miniature playing cards, *left*, tied with a loop of twine, help guests keep track of which wine glass is theirs. **A self-service bar**, *right*, is set up apart from the buffet table on a sturdy built-in bookcase out of the way of traffic.

Design Details

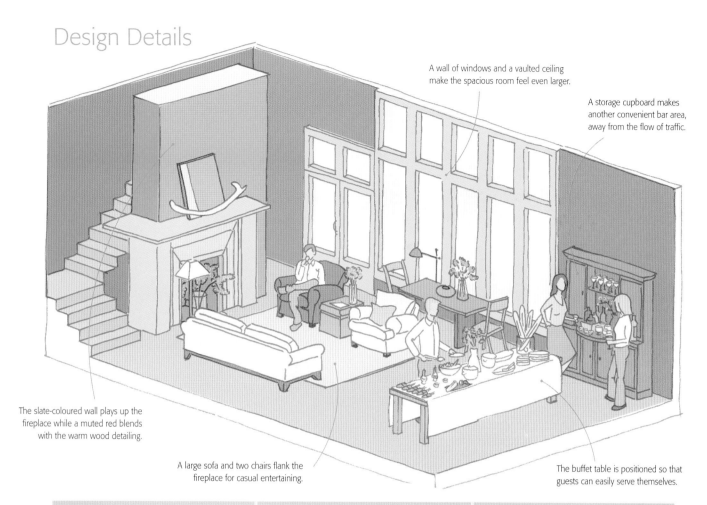

A wall of windows and a vaulted ceiling make the spacious room feel even larger.

A storage cupboard makes another convenient bar area, away from the flow of traffic.

The slate-coloured wall plays up the fireplace while a muted red blends with the warm wood detailing.

A large sofa and two chairs flank the fireplace for casual entertaining.

The buffet table is positioned so that guests can easily serve themselves.

Colour Palette

Contrasting colour schemes can be a powerful addition to spaces with dramatic architectural features. Here, a custom-mixed slate hue surrounds a stately fireplace, and saturated red ochre on the walls helps it stand out in contrast. Red, a welcoming colour that's said to stimulate the appetite, highlights the tones of the warm wood trim. If you choose strong colours, keep it simple with no more than two hues of the same intensity.

Room Plan

A "great room" is at its greatest when furnishings are arranged to offer several "rooms" within the room. This layout makes buffet-style entertaining effortless. Plenty of seating and well-placed tables for setting down plates and drinks are essential. In this space, comfortable upholstered pieces flank the fireplace. The table itself is set in the centre for easy navigation, with room to move around it and a convenient set-up of dinner plates, serving pieces, and cutlery. A serve-yourself bar makes use of an out-of-the-way wall and shelf.

Materials

Douglas fir This dense, versatile, and economical softwood is highly resistant to warping and splitting.

Curly redwood Cut from the base of a redwood tree and distinguished by its dramatic grain, curly redwood is often reserved for interior detailing.

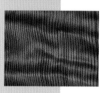

Faux suede Prized for its supple texture and durability, faux suede looks and feels like real suede but is actually a washable synthetic fabric.

Making the Most of a Small Space

A dining area in a small or dual-purpose room requires creativity and ingenuity in space planning. You can make a petite setting seem larger while still preserving its charm by choosing adaptable furniture, simple accessories, and storage that balances practicality with good looks.

Eating in spaces other than traditional dining rooms is sometimes necessary, often pleasant, but not always practical. If your "dining room" is really just a dining area that also doubles as a work space between meals, a layout planned for flexibility is essential. The small dining area in this eat-in kitchen is a good example. Furnished with simple handsome chairs and a sturdy table scaled to the size of the room, the space doesn't feel cluttered with furniture but keeps the focus on the activity at hand. The table is large enough to accommodate diverse pursuits, from paying bills or writing letters to cooking or grabbing a bite to eat. Spread with a crisp white linen cloth, it becomes an elegant stage for an intimate dinner. The comfortable, curved-back chairs are an equally good choice for long dinners or hours spent working at the computer.

A small space can seem pleasantly full if the elements in it are well distributed. Thoughtful organization of neat displays makes a wall filled with both office supplies and tableware visually harmonious. The built-in shelving is a practical yet decorative background that creates a smooth transition in style and mood from dining to work space.

A whimsical wire "clipboard", *left*, turns notes and daily reminders into playful flourishes. Hung low, within easy reach for adding or removing messages, it achieves the decorative effect of a chandelier. **A combined dining-work space**, *right*, is carved out of a kitchen corner. Books and dishes fill the shelves, carrying the colours of the table upwards and unifying the room.

Open shelves framing a built-in work station serve as both an informal china cupboard and a bookcase. All-white dinner and serving pieces make virtue of necessity by doubling as display in the small room. Items used every day such as plates, cups, saucers, and bowls are arranged on lower shelves for easy access, while less frequently used platters and cake stands are stored higher up. A simple chain of paper clips hung vertically can be sculptural as well as functional – serving as a convenient and clever place to hang notes and reminders.

A black-and-white map, *left*, set in a slender matt black frame, leans against a patterned bulletin board, creating a pleasing eye-level display for diners. **Functional pieces**, *above*, like informal dinnerware and a black-and-white clock, maintain the limited colour scheme and keep the shelves looking tidy and unified.

Colour Palette

A simple scheme of white, black, and natural wood creates a sense of tidiness in this small hardworking room. The white china, linen, and chairs unify the space while making it seem larger. Black is used in patterns that boldly define zones for specific uses. The block print on the tablecloth and the checked bulletin board delineate areas for eating and working. Touches of warm wood and brick on the walls add textural impact. A set of rose-coloured stemware provides just enough colour to punctuate the graphic black and white.

Materials

Brick Exposed, aged brick walls give a room old-fashioned charm. Their rough texture and varied colours provide a time-worn contrast to smooth, natural wood shelves and crisp white painted furniture. Left bare, brick walls add an exterior flourish, creating a link to the outdoors.

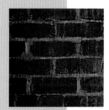

Natural wood Unfinished wood provides a neutral backdrop, offering unlimited possibilities for decorating around it. Dining room necessities like china and sparkling glass look beautiful against natural wood.

China White china is both functional and decorative. A collection of monochromatic china, artfully arranged, can make a dramatic yet soothing statement in a room. In a small room with limited wall space, judiciously placed china can replace artwork as an expression of personal taste.

Room Service

Some of the most memorable meals are the ones you eat in a dining space of your own invention. Create a table-away-from-the-table in a favourite reading nook or with a lavish tray in bed.

It can be a wonderful indulgence to tuck into a meal in a cosy window seat, or any other spot in the house where eating is usually off limits. Re-create the luxury of hotel room service and serve up a feast of favourite delicacies on a pretty dining tray. Choose an imaginative carrier, such as a large shopping basket, an enamelled steel pail, or an old-fashioned picnic hamper, for the rest of your dining accoutrements. With compact and portable serving pieces, it's easy to have your own movable feast.

A stack of white hat boxes, *left*, lined with linen, makes perfect portable storage for breakfast essentials. A stack of two or three brings items up to table height. A toast rack, *above*, puts reading and writing materials at the ready. A sun-filled window seat, *right*, provides a quiet perch for an elegant breakfast.

A weathered wooden picture frame, *below*, inset with a page from a road atlas offers a witty take on one of life's simplest pleasures: a breakfast tray in bed. In fact, almost any flat, sturdy object can be employed as an amusing serving tray for a special meal. **A kitchen island**, *right*, also works as a table with plenty of elbow room for two. A shelf mounted on the wall behind the cooker holds cooking supplies and puts utensils within easy reach. **Wicker baskets**, *below right*, keep kitchen and dining necessities, such as place mats, tidy and turn them into a handsome still-life display.

How to Find More Space

When you make space for the small essentials of dining, you not only reduce clutter, you make dining more pleasurable. There are clever ways to carve space out of even the tiniest of kitchens and to make use of the bounty of a larger area. The wall behind a cooker is a perfect place to hang a storage shelf or rack. A large expanse of wall can become a hardworking message centre. Setting up glassware on a sideboard helps keep a crowded china cupboard tidy. Baskets for place mats, napkins, and cutlery alleviate cluttered drawers and restore order to worktops and cupboards. Armed with these solutions, you might even find enough room for a kitchen garden of fragrant herbs.

Waxed-paper–lined newspaper, *left*, makes simple individual serving cones for popcorn. Tucked into a clear glass bowl, they're easy to transport and save on washing up after a snack. **A kitchen blackboard**, *above*, makes fast work of writing the shopping list. Clothes pegs clipped along a metal bar keep recipes and menus organized and handy for noting ingredients you need to buy.

colour

As the place in our homes where a blend of flavours and an abundance of textures are most appreciated, dining rooms afford a special opportunity to use colour freely. A rich backdrop of claret red or a vibrant wall of celadon green infuses a space with colour that invigorates the senses. As a starting point when decorating a dining room, choose hues that enhance the menu or inspire conversation.

In the days of the Chinese silk trade, sea captains brought coloured silk and hand-painted paper back from the Orient to grace their dining room walls. Dining rooms decorated in crimson, amber, or gold were considered ideal for enjoying meals and entertaining guests. If you're not sure about using a lot of colour, mix in a few vivid hues against a more neutral base (much like matching a brilliant jumper with a favourite faded pair of jeans). The dining room is a natural place to try out different colour combinations because accessories alter its palette almost daily, depending on the event, the menu, the flowers, or the season. In fact, since the table is the focus of a dining room, changing its colour scheme (and the room's atmosphere) is easier and more affordable than it is in almost any other space in the home.

To co-ordinate your dining room, divide it into two parts: the table settings and the room at large. Work outwards from the table. Do you prefer to bring in colour through tableware and linen, offsetting it with a neutral backdrop, or do you like a simple white table against colourful furnishings and walls? Is yours a room used for parties that can shoulder dramatic tones, or one used for informal fare that asks for a light, casual atmosphere? Even a favourite regional cuisine can inspire your colour choices. If you like the flavours of Provence, sunflower yellows and pale lavender can evoke that region for you every day. Or you might use ochre and olive green to give your dining space the glow of a Tuscan villa.

Colour also influences atmosphere. There's lots of conventional wisdom about colour: red is proven to stimulate appetite and conversation; pink is said to be flattering and offer a sense of security; orange is warm and lively; violet stimulates creativity; cool blue quenches thirst. But perhaps personal wisdom is even better. Any colour that puts you at ease can work for you in some proportion. Let one major hue blend within a range of accents for flavour and spice. And don't forget to stir the pot once in a while.

Dress the dining table with the colours you love, whether muted or bold. Collect a range of table linen, dishes, glassware, and centrepieces in your favourite hues.

Setting for the Season

Every season has its colour. Using a seasonal palette creates a welcoming backdrop to the meal, just as using in-season ingredients accentuates the meal itself. For example, the glowing, natural hues or burnished golds, oranges, and fiery reds clearly invoke autumn and its bountiful harvest.

There's no mistaking the colours of autumn. Nature takes out all the guesswork, providing a perfect palette of rich earth tones that offer countless possible combinations. In fact, basing a colour scheme on natural hues is a good idea in almost any season, whether you favour the sea and sky blues of a summer beach setting or the snowy white and evergreen of winter slopes. But there's something especially enticing about an autumnal colour scheme in the dining room. Begin with a single hue as a wall colour; any autumnal shade, from pale butternut to deep ochre, acts as an invitation to relax and share conversation. Bring variations of the same glowing tone to curtains and upholstery, and then assemble accessories and decorations in accent colours that take the mood from everyday to entertaining.

Since sun-drenched hues of yellow and red also happen to stimulate the appetite, they're naturals, not only at big feasts but also at family gatherings throughout the year. Gracing any table, these colours conjure bounty and fulfilment. For a fresh look, add touches of creamy white – on the table, in architectural details, or with painted furniture – to keep the tones of this warm palette distinct.

Bittersweet sprigs, *left*, give an all-white display of china a touch of autumnal colour. **A seasonal table**, *right*, takes its cue from autumn colours at their peak. Amber glassware, persimmon napkins, and an orange linen runner transform a set of white dinnerware into a warm, colourful table setting. A pencil and note card mark each place setting, inspiring guests to give thanks.

In this warm and festive dining room, a creamy white table setting complements the butternut colour of the walls. An informal centrepiece of gourds and bittersweet, balanced by chargers set with glowing candles, beautifully enhances the warm palette while bringing the table to life. Blocks of colour create contrast on the table: a wide nubby linen runner layered over a white tablecloth adds a touch of burnt orange, and napkins in a deeper shade of persimmon help define each place setting.

A note card and pencil, *above*, give guests the chance to express their thoughts on an event such as a birthday or christening. The host can later read aloud the sentiments as part of the celebration. **Basic white accents**, *right*, from the tablecloth and dishes to the sheer curtains at the windows, keep the seasonal palette fresh and modern. Amber glassware, glowing candles, and glazed earthenware link the table settings to the wall colour.

Colour Palette

It's no coincidence that a warm palette of butternut, wheat, and persimmon is thought to stimulate the appetite: all these colours suggest foods. This colour scheme recalls the most bountiful time of the year, organized neatly in the warm zone of the colour wheel between the hot shades that connote summer and the cool ones that evoke winter. Here, the palette begins with the golden butternut walls and is carried through to the earthenware, amber glassware, and table linen. White accents dress up the room without seeming too formal.

What would a family celebration be without a children's table? Make kids feel as special as the grown-ups by bringing colour to their dining table, but in a simpler way. A polished wooden table fits into any colour scheme perfectly and makes wiping away the wayward mashed potatoes a breeze. A gourd or small pumpkin as a centrepiece echoes the larger arrangement on the adults' table, and the look of amber glassware is matched at the kids' table with orange plastic tumblers. Clever place mats, in the form of white sketchpads, make the tiny table look as fresh and modern as its large-scale counterpart – and keep children busy when the main course is finished.

Lay a children's table, *left*, in a streamlined version of the grown-ups', with durable deep-dish plates. **Wooden animal name tags**, *above*, guide children to their seats. White sketchpads and a plentiful supply of crayons keep little hands busy and the table looking fresh.

Materials

Ironstone A durable fired clay pottery that was developed in England in the nineteenth century, ironstone takes its name from the traces of powdered iron rumoured to be included in its patented formula. Generally thicker than china, ironstone is available in a variety of glazes, colours, and styles.

Raw linen Woven in varying grades, linen's texture ranges from rough to very fine. Table linens in a coarser weave make good runners. Delicate gauges drape well as formal tablecloths or dinner napkins. The unfinished edges of raw linen textiles impart a natural homespun feeling.

Rush A type of marsh plant with hollow cylindrical reeds that, when dried, are used for weaving seats or braiding place mats. Wooden ladder-back chairs and rocking chairs in Colonial and Shaker styles are commonly fitted with rush seats.

Club Colours

A hallway or alcove in rich, refined red has the air of a Hollywood supper club. Furnished with a gentleman's bar and leather upholstery, it becomes the perfect stage for pre-dinner drinks.

Create the atmosphere of an old-fashioned Hollywood club by painting the walls of an alcove or small room in oxblood red. Deep, warm colours, especially on the wall, make a room feel intimate and theatrical. Since dark polished wood and leather have red undertones, they work especially well with this strong colour scheme. Add a well-stocked bar, some framed black-and-white prints, and bright white trim (which helps to tailor a deep colour). Keep polished bar tools, mixers, and bitters close at hand, and you're fully outfitted for a classic cocktail party.

Manhattans served in martini glasses, *left*, sparkle on top of mirrored coasters and trays. **Chilled caviar**, *above*, and toasted bread are an elegant cocktail hour offering. **A drinks cabinet**, *right*, is fully outfitted for classic cocktails.

How to Dress Up a Table

Use colour to give a dining table a quick change of style. Start with high-quality basics: a fine linen tablecloth and cutlery that's at least 18/8 stainless steel for durability and a nice balance in the hand. Then personalize each setting with a place card, favour, and napkin ring that reflect the occasion. Take cues from the colours around you. Place settings needn't be elaborate. As long as they're festive, they will make your guests feel special.

Amber settings, *opposite*, are perfect at harvest time. Small pumpkins hold place cards; rickrack napkin rings and sprigs of bittersweet decorate the table. **Candy-striped paper**, *left*, wraps individual cakes and small gifts for a surprise party. **Pomegranates**, *below left*, along with tiny ornament place card holders, Christmas crackers, and red dishes, greet guests with colours of the season. **Sparkler favours**, *below*, ring in the New Year alongside napkins tied with witty clocks. Rosemary garlands and votives compose a memorable centrepiece.

Warm colours

We've selected a range of warm colours, which work especially well for dining spaces, in hues chosen to invigorate the senses, inspire the appetite, and enhance intimate gatherings. Reds are said to stimulate both appetite and conversation, making them ideal for dining spaces. Pink, a softer form of red, flatters the complexion and is thought to offer a sense of security. Combine saturated warm tones, such as plum and aubergine, with pale tints of creamy neutrals to create a colour scheme that's nuanced and balanced.

Neutral colours

Neutral walls and furnishings in a dining space make a room feel spacious and allow you to add accessories of any colour. Our palette of neutrals accommodates both warm and cool accents. Combine cool neutrals such as grey and white with blues and greens. Pair warm hues such as taupe with fiery reds and oranges.

Cool colours

Favoured for their ability to make surroundings feel calm and refined, cool colours are often the hues of choice in dining spaces. Our selection of cool colours draws on the range of blues and greens found in nature. Pale colours such as sky blue and celadon green are ideal for a tranquil dining room, and look particularly elegant when mixed with lots of white or with dark chocolate browns for contrast. Fresh green always goes well in a kitchen and its association with the outdoors lends a sense of warmth to the cool surfaces of many kitchen materials.

How to co-ordinate colours

We've created this guide to help you choose colours for your dining space. Use core or basic colours for foundation pieces such as walls and furnishings, and layer co-ordinating table accessories and details in accent hues to create an enticing palette.

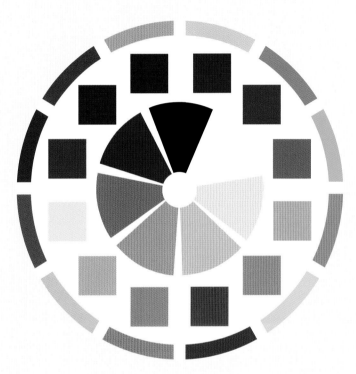

Core colours, shown in the centre of the wheel, include neutrals in shades of stone, brown, and black. Used on walls, ceilings, or floors, core colours can be a canvas for colourful accessories or the basis for a monochromatic palette. Wood finishes for many table and chair options fall into this core category.

Basic colours, in the middle ring, make a more dramatic dining room statement. Suitable for walls, curtains, or a suite of chairs, each colour is presented in a quadrant of rich hues that are tonally similar. If you paint your walls in one of these colours, choose accessories in adjacent hues to add depth to your palette.

Accent colours, in the outer ring, are ideal for accessories and display pieces. These vibrant hues give a room character and personality. Brightly coloured table linen, glassware, cushions, centrepieces, and rugs can be chosen according to the season, the mood that you want to create, or the occasion that you're celebrating.

texture

Furnishings in a dining space should not only be visually striking but also feel good to the touch. In a dining space, the fragrance and flavour of food, the clatter of conversation, and the flicker of candlelight all stir the senses. However, texture is what gives a room soul. Texture can be thought of in terms of surface quality, smooth or rough, or with regard to depth, whether bristled or plush. No matter which textures you like, the experience of touch should be thoughtfully addressed through the fabrics, the finishes, even the dishes you choose.

or sheer curtains to create mottled shadows when light shines through them. The glittering crystals or wrought iron of a chandelier, shelves laden with smooth sculptural serving pieces, and the repeated patterns of cane or bentwood chairs all invite attention and captivate the eye.

Marked textural contrasts are perhaps the most interesting. The wear of a rough surface is even more pronounced when offset by the sheen of a sleek one, so a distressed sideboard is never more attractive than when it stands next to a highly polished table. Likewise, marble worktops and

Like some of the most satisfying meals, a thoughtfully composed dining space boasts a rich combination of textures that stimulates the senses and warms the heart.

Everyone wants to sit down at a table replete with dishes, glassware, centrepieces, and linen that indulge the senses. When laying the dining room table, first consider the materials that you will touch directly: the smooth glass of stemware, the soft linen of a cloth napkin, the cool metal of cutlery, the polished wood of a sideboard. The effect of each texture alone is small, but in combination they add up to a well-rounded sensory experience that makes your guests feel relaxed, comfortable, and happy.

While the table may be the centre of attention, it's important to infuse the whole room with texture. You might try matchstick window blinds

stainless steel appliances might be matched in a kitchen with a gently worn pine table for an intriguing balance of warm and cool textures.

Texture can draw attention to real temperature differences, too. Depending on the event or the season, you can change the way everything feels in your dining space. When it's cold outside, dress the table with a luxurious fabric like velvet or wool to convey warmth. In the hotter months, lightweight cotton or even an uncovered table help to keep the mood light and fresh.

Whatever effect you want to achieve, a blend of textures creates a room that you, your family, and your guests will appreciate at every meal.

Mixing Old and New

A kitchen-dining room that combines the new with the weathered and antique is welcoming and timeless. Defy the expected by setting gently worn, rustic furniture against the sleek finishes of a modern kitchen. When it comes to texture, opposites always attract.

The beauty of timeworn furniture is often appreciated the most when contrasting with something new. If you have an heirloom table or favourite vintage piece, the best home for it might be amongst contemporary surroundings. When mixing old and new, the secret lies in how you balance things.

In a kitchen-dining room, vintage pieces on one side of the room and modern ones on the other can have great synergy. Use wood, with all its surface variety, to provide a textural starting point that you can weave throughout the space. Consider how textures change from the hardworking kitchen area to the relaxed dining area, and plan accordingly; look for finishes that are appealing in both. For example, in this kitchen-dining room, the sealed butcher's block worktop and distressed wood dining table create a duet of textures across the space.

Soft, similar colours throughout show texture to its best advantage. Antique furniture appears to get a facelift just by being set against a clean, painted backdrop. The colour palette in this spacious room smooths the transition from the rich woods of the dresser and refectory table to the cool stainless steel of the range and sink fittings.

Simple white bowls, *left*, provide smooth contrast when set against textural place mats and a vintage wooden table top. **A distressed cupboard**, *right*, offers a window into a collection of china and vintage linen. A long cushioned bench plays against expectations as it stands in for dining chairs.

What pleases the hand usually pleases the eye as well. A decor that favours texture makes a kitchen-dining room atmosphere even more pleasurable. Here, the mellow distressed wood of antique furnishings provides a relaxing view for busy cooks, and the satiny white paint on a kitchen island underscores fresh, simply prepared food. You can also choose to highlight texture by opting for a bit of the unexpected. Notice how the glossy white armchair sits brightly at the foot of the table and bridges the natural transition from dining area to kitchen.

Stone slabs, *above*, set on top of the smooth wooden butcher's block, make place mats for kids to garden, colour, and draw on. **Wide-plank wood floors**, *right*, are stained in a high-gloss deep walnut, creating a staging ground for the many other tactile surfaces in both the kitchen and dining areas.

Texture can punctuate space as well as define it. Here a colour-bound sisal rug is a mediating texture between the worn vintage furniture and the new wood floor beneath. The material on a central kitchen island serves the intentions of both sides of the room: the thick butcher's block is ideal for preparing food, but it's also a good table top on which to have breakfast, do homework, or make crafts.

Texture is visible in the details: facets of glass and crystal, the geometry of seating and cupboards.

Pattern, too, can constitute texture. Open wine storage and deep shelves fronting the kitchen island create an interesting visual dimension, as do vertical slats in the chair backs, wood panelling, and mullioned cupboards. These are the ordered, repeated textures that lend a room rhythm. Crystal droplets on an ornate chandelier, conversely, provide free-form texture, glittering all day in changing patterns of light.

Stainless steel appliances, *left*, and freshly painted chairs combine with pleasingly scuffed dining room furniture to give this room a relaxed, casual feeling. **A tassel of shells**, *right*, dresses up a rope tieback – two organic textures stand out against sheer cotton voile curtains.

Design Details

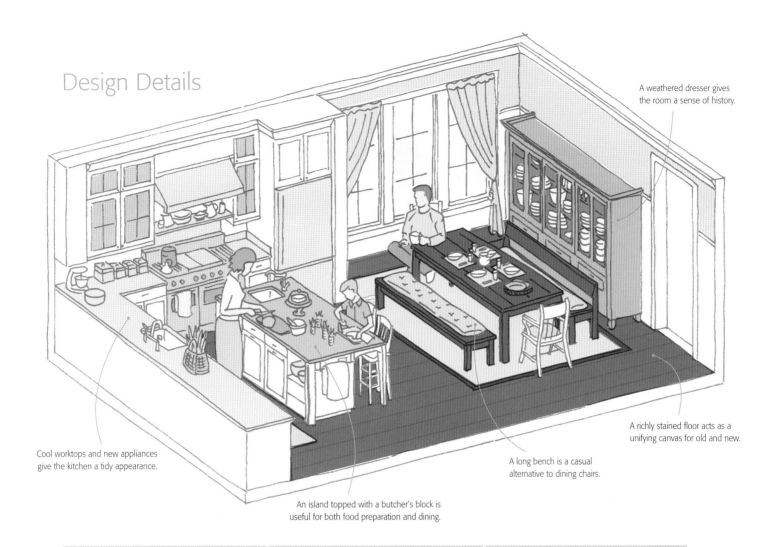

A weathered dresser gives the room a sense of history.

A richly stained floor acts as a unifying canvas for old and new.

Cool worktops and new appliances give the kitchen a tidy appearance.

An island topped with a butcher's block is useful for both food preparation and dining.

A long bench is a casual alternative to dining chairs.

Colour Palette

Colour can be used either to enhance or disguise the differences in contrasting textures. Here, a limited colour palette of pale green, creamy white, and espresso subtly emphasizes a wide range of materials from distressed wood to stainless steel. A natural pairing, brown and green complement each other's essential qualities: brown highlights green's freshness, while green brings out the depth and warmth of brown.

Room Plan

Finely finished spaces can combine many textures and still appear cohesive. This space employs classic texture contrasts (old and new) as an informal divider between cooking and eating areas. Each "room" expresses half of a texture pair: smooth, sleek kitchen fixtures versus rustic, weathered dining room furniture. Because wood is an element displayed throughout, the parts make up a visual whole. Lighting joins the textural mix, with industrial-style pendants over the workspaces and vines of crystals around the dining room chandelier.

Materials

Distressed paint Gently worn, original paint is a desirable furniture finish, but everyday kitchen cupboards should get a clear coat of glaze to protect against nicks.

Vintage linen Prized for their beautifully faded patterns and timeworn softness, vintage textiles have become collectable.

Butcher's block Often made from narrow strips of maple laminated together, this makes a thick, durable surface for food preparation.

Hearthside Dining

Indulge a passion for luxury by having a picnic indoors. Spread the table with a lavish shawl and surround yourself with layers of soft texture: a shag-pile rug, cushions, and a cosy throw.

There are many places to have a quick snack or a casual meal, but none is more inviting than the living room rug and the spot near the fireplace. Kick off your shoes and set the coffee table with things that welcome the touch: a fringed pashmina shawl, nubby linen napkins, cool polished cutlery. You might find pretty accessories made of shell or quartz to add a bit of shimmer to the table, or a ridged wooden bowl to impart a sense of warmth. Bring the lighting down low with candles arranged on the floor, and pull up soft cushions as seating for two.

A textural place setting, *left*, shows pleasurable contrasts: polished shell chargers, soft linen napkins, and mother-of-pearl salt and pepper shakers. **Votives nestled amid pine cones**, *above*, make a glowing, organic vignette. **Soft loomed wool floor cushions**, *right*, set on a shag-pile rug, provide seating at the coffee table.

A bounty of artichokes, *left*, is arranged like a bouquet of flowers and set in a coarse-grained wooden bowl. **The cool shells of blown eggs**, *top*, are a smooth counterpoint to the gauze that lines their bowls. Cluster quail eggs in the middle of the table for the greatest impact, or set one or two eggs in a salt cellar at each place setting. **A single chive blossom**, *above*, rests in a shiny stone bowl as a striking minimalist table decoration.

How to Create Natural Centrepieces

A botanical centrepiece is an inspired way to bring perfect proportion, natural texture, and fresh colour to your dining table, but this time-tested strategy need not involve a vase of freshly cut flowers. Consider the shingled surface of an artichoke, the smooth ridges of a pumpkin. Even the scarlet skin of a single shapely apple can bring an element of interest – and the unexpected – to your table. As you assemble your centrepiece, play with contrasts and look at nature's offerings in a new way. If the shape of a piece of driftwood and the sheen of a river stone take your breath away, why not pair them up in the middle of your dining room table for all to admire.

Gourds and pumpkins, *left*, are elevated to centrepiece status when studded with branches of bittersweet and displayed on a footed ceramic cake stand. **A weathered wooden bottle tray**, *above*, salvaged from a Coca-Cola bottling plant, makes the perfect portable table-top arrangement. The compartments are filled with all the necessities for a romantic dinner: glass votive cubes, bud vases, extra candles, and gleaming cutlery.

furnishings

Decorating the dining room once involved complex rules of etiquette. But with today's casual lifestyle, meals are a movable feast guided by simplicity and ease. The dining area is just as often in the kitchen or "great room" as it is in a formal dining room. In all these spaces, you want furniture that can be fine-tuned to accommodate afternoon snacks and family dinners, or to seat a crowd.

Choosing a table comes first, and it can be hard to find one tailored to all your needs. As an added challenge, the modern-day dining room is now a

(16–18 in), and style choices abound. You can narrow the field by focussing on the kind of atmosphere you'd like for your dining room. Benches and stools are more casual, loose-covered or upholstered seats can look a bit more formal. In between, there are farmhouse and wicker chairs with loose cushions, small bent-wood bistro chairs, and large leather armchairs. The simpler the table, the easier it is to pair with any chair style. Don't be afraid to combine textures and materials: mismatched chairs and tables make great eclectic dining partners.

The best dining room furniture accommodates many occasions – a simple family meal, a romantic dinner for two, a small celebration, or a grand one.

place to pay bills and do homework or projects as much as it is a place to eat. For shape, consult the room itself. If it's small or square, try a round table to maximize the number of seats. If your dining room is spacious, opt for a long rectangular table to fill the room. Tables with removable leaves are perfect space savers when you entertain often but don't have room for an everyday table for twelve. No matter what table shape you choose, find a size that allows at least 60 cm (2 ft) for each person's place setting.

Comfortable seating is basic to a well-furnished dining room, but it doesn't have to look basic. The ideal seat height for a dining chair is 40–45 cm

Storage comes next. For storing dishes, cutlery, linen, and serving pieces, you can choose from almost any type of cupboard or open shelves. Shelving looks the most modern. Free-standing cupboards always look classic (and hide their contents for a tidy outward appearance). Be creative in recasting furniture: a cedar chest for table linen, a glass apothecary case for china.

In all of your choices, remember this: rooms evolve. Don't be shy about adding new elements, trying different arrangements, or switching things around. Trust your own style and follow your own rules. If your dining room makes you happy, chances are it will make your guests happy, too.

Versatile Dining Room Classics

A farmhouse kitchen conjures comforting images: a generous hearth to sit by, lovingly prepared meals, and favourite furnishings that have withstood the test of time. Create a country atmosphere in your dining space with furniture that's designed for lasting comfort.

A farmhouse kitchen may be the design equivalent of comfort food. Whether the table is in the kitchen or the kitchen spills out into another dining area, the familiar ritual of preparing and sharing food is the main ingredient in this pleasurable environment. No matter what space you have, if you're aiming for this versatile look, it's best to start with the main piece of furniture: an ample table – one that is honestly hewn and simply shaped. If you can find an appropriate vintage piece, its pleasingly worn surface and sense of history will bring added rewards to the room.

It's helpful to compare farmhouse table styles, since there are many interpretations. Rustic versions are made from softwoods such as pine, hardwoods such as maple, or fruitwoods such as cherry or pear. They may have a charmingly uneven surface and narrow width, which keeps dining companions nearer and suits smaller spaces. New tables have an even, wide surface, which allows for more seats at the table and more room for serving pieces. Some much-coveted versions have pull-out breadboards and artfully turned legs. Whether it's a genuine antique or a quality reproduction, all farmhouse furnishings have a sturdy, timeless profile that only improves with wear.

A hand-planed farmhouse table, *left*, is a design that's been around for more than three centuries. Incredibly sturdy, it's ideal for casual family meals. **A vintage milk carrier**, *right*, makes a perfect wine-holder centrepiece.

Finding the right mix of seating is just as important as choosing the right table when creating a relaxed and informal atmosphere. You'll want comfortable dining chairs for leisurely suppers, high stools at a kitchen island for socializing or eating breakfast, and soft chairs nearby for simply relaxing. Farmhouse tables go well with any type of dining chair, from classic to modern. Here, a pair of wing chairs updates the traditional form with woven seagrass and complements a set of country-style dining chairs nearby. You can create a similar pairing of harmonious styles by placing two upholstered wing chairs at the heads of the table to soften the setting.

A basket of peaches, *above*, makes a simple yet beautiful centrepiece. **A sun-filled room**, *right*, is furnished with casual comfort in mind. The curves and textures of the chairs are as pleasant to the touch as they are to the eye.

Inherently suited to both entertaining and everyday dining, this layout is filled with ideas for putting every inch of your own dining room to good use. The centre of the room is devoted to a long table for family suppers; chairs are pulled up to the hearth for intimate dinners; and bar-height seats make the island an extra dining table.

Modern farmhouse style relies on sturdy, comfortable furniture updated with a bit of flair.

A fine congregating point on its own, the durable butcher's block surface of the island helps with both serving and entertaining duties. Placing hors d'oeuvres here, buffet style, is less formal than passing platters. Notice, too, how the gracious table settings emphasize both the informal and the epicurean. Heavy cotton tea towels used for both place mats and napkins share the durable characteristics of the table, chairs, and crockery.

A generously scaled table, *left*, can be so prominent that it becomes part of the dining room's architecture. Accents of white soften its presence and lift the atmosphere of the room. **The kitchen island**, *right*, is perfectly situated for easy entertaining; a simple cheese course is set out on worn breadboards.

Design Details

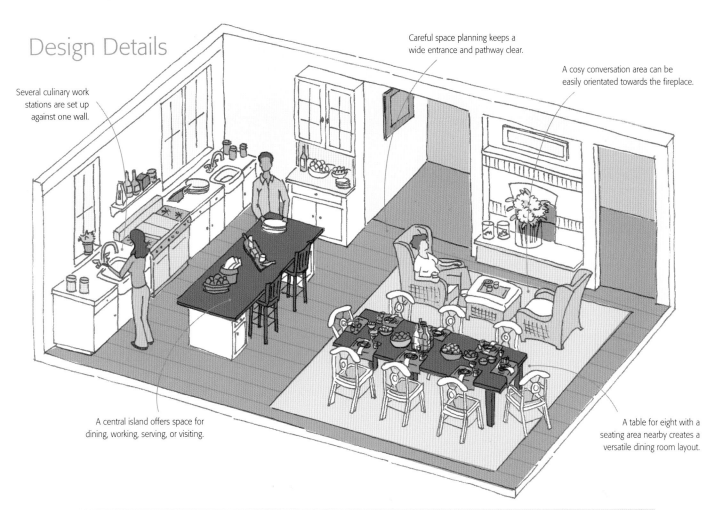

Several culinary work stations are set up against one wall.

Careful space planning keeps a wide entrance and pathway clear.

A cosy conversation area can be easily orientated towards the fireplace.

A central island offers space for dining, working, serving, or visiting.

A table for eight with a seating area nearby creates a versatile dining room layout.

Colour Palette

If you love farmhouse ambience in general and natural materials in particular, you can invoke both in your own home with a palette of camel, linen white, and berry red. Here, camel and white create a seamless transition from one part of the room to the other. Simple accents in berry red warm up an otherwise neutral palette. Red and white always make an arresting combination that enlivens a space and gives it cheerful personality.

Room Plan

You might be surprised to realize that there are a total of twelve chairs in this space. Distributed in an approximate triangle across the open plan, each of the three seating areas is angled with a view onto the kitchen. Arranged around the fireplace, a pair of seagrass wing chairs forms an intimate and cosy seating area. A table for eight is set perpendicular to the kitchen area to make the most of the floor space. Two bar chairs slide out from the kitchen island and stay tucked under when not in use. Lots of natural light floods the room for a sunny atmosphere.

Materials

Jute The softest of all the raw natural fibres, jute is strong enough to be used for rugs. Natural jute ranges in colour from light tan to dark brown.

Tea cloths These absorbent cotton towels are meant for culinary use, but their bold patterns make them a nice accent for the dining table.

Seagrass This fibre comes from several aquatic plant species. When densely woven into rugs or other furnishings, seagrass has a subtle green tint and smooth surface.

outdoors

Entertaining alfresco requires only two more elements than indoor dining: a comfortable place to sit outdoors and fine weather. Whether a picnic by a small pond, a knapsack lunch at the end of a long hike, or a slope-side snack during an afternoon of skiing, the combination of good food and fresh air makes a lasting impression. There are few rules when it comes to dining outdoors; settings can be formal or whimsical, simple or sumptuous. All that's needed for open-air dining is a little imagination, some sturdy household goods, and a handy bag.

and many materials are sun- and rain-friendly. Canvas is woven tightly to provide some weather resistance, making it ideal for upholstery. Batiks and woven cottons, such as twill, soften with repeated washings and fade elegantly in the sun. Natural linen and translucent gauze make inspired curtains that can be inexpensively replaced each season. Use fabric to make an outdoor space feel even more like a dining room: hang panels around the perimeter of a veranda, drawing them to filter the midday sun and pulling them back for a view of the sunset.

Entertaining outdoors lets you relax, be creative, and enjoy both the planning and the party. Create an outdoor dining room that feels far away from the everyday.

A wide stretch of lawn makes a perfect picnic spot, but for a more permanent warm-weather dining set-up, let the seasons for outdoor dining or the year-round climate guide your decisions. Outdoor dining furniture should stand up to the elements, which means choosing materials that weather well. Look for wooden furniture that is sealed, and varieties like cedar, teak, and bamboo, which resist warping in moisture. Choose rust-resistant metal furniture, and use weatherproof exterior paints to protect rattan or wicker.

You'll want to be practical with the core pieces, but your outdoor space doesn't have to look rugged. Textiles add luxury to an outdoor setting,

Whether you prefer to serve lunch dockside or to entertain at a long table under a pergola, your meal will be made more pleasant by fewer trips back and forth to the kitchen. Set up a covered étagère to hold portable containers of cutlery, napkins, candles – everything you need to lay the table. This piece can also be used as a serving-and-clearing station throughout the meal. Plan ahead for lighting in case the celebration lasts past dusk. String up tiny lights or hang lanterns from the veranda ceiling, a tree limb, or any over-head structure, to serve as an outdoor chandelier. Make sure there's enough light to keep the table illuminated, and let the starry sky do the rest.

Set up for Summer

Take advantage of the charms of eating outdoors, and set up the veranda for summer dining. Borrow some of the comforts of indoor entertaining to create a setting that's part picnic, all pleasure.

A veranda links the outdoors with the rest of the house. Set yours up as a warm-weather dining room with plenty of comfortable cushions to encourage relaxation. Let comfort and easy maintenance be your guide when choosing furnishings.

Outfit an étagère with weatherproof baskets to make the perfect outdoor storage unit for tableware and candles, as well as newspapers and favourite books. Here, foldable all-weather teak garden chairs are furnished with plump, washable cushions for indoor and outdoor comfort.

Enjoy the time-honoured tradition, *left*, of dining on the veranda. **Brew sun tea,** *above*, in acrylic glassware that won't break (or sweat in the sun). **String up voile curtains,** *right*, to shade the sun, then relax with iced tea and good friends.

Bringing Home the Beach

There are some foods that simply are meant to be eaten outdoors, at the height of their flavour and season. Set a table outside and let a party linger for hours over a meal that's fresh, simple, and abundant. Sun up or down, a breezy, open-air setting makes beautiful weather the guest of honour.

Whenever you head outdoors for an afternoon feast, memories are in the making. Barbecues are popular meals in fine weather and the perfect choice for family gatherings. If seafood is a summer favourite, you don't have to live by the beach to enjoy the informal atmosphere of an oceanside grille. Re-create the seashore wherever you are by setting the table with sailing whites, ocean blues, and bold nautical stripes. Eat on a patio, veranda, or lawn, or in an open pool house decorated for the occasion. A calming palette of blue and white, combined with elegant beachcomber finds, captures the sunny mood of a summer by the sea.

Begin with an abundance of white to keep the atmosphere crisp and fresh in the afternoon heat. Use a neat white linen tablecloth as a backdrop, and look for place mats, seat cushions, and place cards in mix-and-match patterns. Layer clear blue glass or acrylic with simple white dinnerware. Under summer skies, accents of blue in furnishings and tableware suggest the sea by day and complement the colours of the horizon at dusk.

Lobster-crackers, *left*, are bundled with picks and lashed together with rope tied in sailors' knots. **A favourite block-printed fabric**, *right*, is laminated to make practical place mats; durable blue acrylic tableware is dressed up with neat white plates and bowls. Layered in seafaring blues and white, the table looks inviting and seasonal.

A table doesn't need a centrepiece to create a lasting impression. Dress up an outdoor dining room with nautical touches like the ones shown here. Use white canvas curtains to recall a billowy sail. Set the centre of the table with blue votives and use shells as salt and pepper cellars. Complete the theme with place cards folded into paper boats.

Block print cushions, *left*, in varying patterns of blue and white, mix easily with cushions in simple ticking stripes that share the same colours. For outdoor dining, blue cotton fabrics enjoy an especially long life because they fade attractively in the sun. **An antique bookend**, *above*, used as a napkin-holder, echoes the sailing motif. Often, the perfect combination of napkins, place mats, and place cards is all that's needed for a festive outdoor table.

As daylight turns to dusk, pretty blue-painted wicker chairs become more practical. The colour blue has long been considered serene and relaxing, but it is also said to repel insects. Beyond the intimacy of the table, in this expansive garden, a calm blue pool looks even more soothing at night with candles surrounding the perimeter. Lanterns, made by placing votives in cups or paper bags, are easy to make; stabilize the candles with a few inches of sand. Candle torches and tiny seashells filled with lamp oil can be scattered around a patio for added flickers of light.

For perfect dining, day or night, *left*, settings on a poolside table move easily from casual lunch to finer evening fare. **Paper cup votives**, *above*, are pierced with a hole punch to make patterns with pinpoints of light. **Candles around the pool**, *right*, illuminate the evening celebration.

Design Details

Worktop flanking the fireplace serves as a sideboard.

French windows allow the patio space to extend indoors.

Stone walls set apart an outdoor kitchen from the rest of the space.

A rug helps transform an outdoor space into a "room".

Linen and cushioned chairs bring the luxury of indoor dining outdoors.

Colour Palette

Blue and white make a classic combination that can look tailored and formal — or relaxed and sporty. It simply depends on the scale and graphics of the patterns you use. Bold florals or stripes will do the trick for a nautical or tropical look. Patterns layer well in this palette, and varied hues of blue mix well – especially when some are pale and some are deep. Take advantage of candlelight and glassware to make blue sparkle like water in the sun.

Room Plan

You can entertain with ease all summer if you organize your outdoor layout as you would an indoor space, with separate areas for cooking, serving, and eating. The cooking area can be as simple as a portable grille or as elaborate as the built-in unit shown here. Any horizontal surface, whether a folding table or a worktop, can be used as a sideboard. This layout places the outdoor kitchen away from the dining area to keep grille smoke from reaching diners. Lanterns provide ample light for cooking without detracting from the romance of a twilight supper.

Materials

Wicker Created of woven bamboo, cane, rattan, or willow, wicker furnishings are durable enough to stand up to heavy use.

Block prints These fabrics have patterns that are transferred to the material's surface through stamping rather than weaving.

Acrylic Lightweight and impact-resistant, acrylic is perfect for outdoor use. With a variety of colours and styles, acrylic dinnerware can easily accent a casual dinner table.

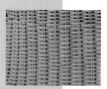

The Perfect Setting

Leave paper napkins on the shelf. An impromptu picnic may be the perfect setting for all the lovely antique tableware you can find – whether at the flea market or hiding in your cutlery drawer.

Place settings have changed since the days when a proper table included sugar tongs, berry spoons, and pickle forks. But fine linen and vintage silver make a spread set on a picnic hamper truly sumptuous. Pull out all the stops and pack a cool repast with all the trimmings that etiquette once required. Forgo paper plates; instead gather crystal stemware, pressed damask, polished silver, and a delicate spray of roses to make dinner on the lawn an event to remember.

A portable butler's pantry, *left*, includes a silver ice bucket, fine wine, and individual servings of gazpacho. **Good china**, *above*, keeps company with heirloom silver tied up with packing twine. **Mix old and new**, *right*, with a favourite vintage clay vase and contemporary tableware.

Dockside Dining

A lazy day by the water is a treat that only gets better when accompanied by a delicious meal. Make a simple summer table graceful with a few clever accessories. Set up provisions in a decorative basket that holds everything you'll need for relaxing until the sun goes down.

When the sky is bright blue, the sun is brilliant, and natural beauty surrounds you, there's no better pleasure than spending the whole day outside – and that includes mealtimes. If your favourite spot at the lake or in the woods is just a short walk from home, why not carry a few dining conveniences with you and have a portable meal ready to serve at your destination? The traditional approach is to put everything you need in a picnic hamper. But choose a modern basket made of wire instead of straw, add a few pretty accessories, and you have something more – ready transport for outdoor dining with flair.

Before you set out for the dock or the beach, make a few indoor preparations. Borrow the cutlery container from the dish rack and fill it with drinks and supplies: it will hook onto most baskets for safe transport. Bundle inexpensive wood or bamboo utensils as a casual substitute for plastic, and add a few extra sets, to keep kids busy digging in the sand. Leave plates behind and wrap sandwiches in paper napkins or generous tea towels (the latter can double as place mats). You might head out beforehand to arrange some floor cushions, a folding table, or a blanket to create an oasis that will be waiting for you.

Wrapped like presents, *left*, sandwiches are kept fresh with a napkin and a twist of twine. **A wire basket**, *right*, serves as a mini-pantry, complete with drinks, a bottle opener (tied on with string,) utensils, dishware, and even its own floral centrepiece of Queen Anne's lace.

Colour Palette

Whether the colours come from nature, in the form of white sands and blue seas, or from fabric and paint, the combination of blue and white can be unabashedly tropical. This classic island colour scheme can stand up to bright sunlight. Near the water or inland, the cooling effect of these two colours makes them a popular choice for warm climates. Accents of stripes, especially in black and white, make the palette more sophisticated and add a touch of the French Riviera.

Materials

Cedar An ideal material for outdoor furniture, such as the occasional table seen here, cedar is a softwood that is naturally resistant to decay and insect damage. It also ages to a beautiful silver grey colour over time.

Sunproof fabric Sunlight can break down fabric and cause it to tear easily, but a new generation of outdoor materials is specially designed to be sunproof, water-resistant, and weatherproof. Usually a tightly woven synthetic blend, sunproof fabrics often mimic the look of canvas or sailcloth.

Terry cloth A cotton fabric with a moisture-absorbing loop pile covering the entire surface on both sides, soft terry cloth is typically used for beach towels, bathrobes, and bath mats. Quick-drying and washable, terry cloth also makes a fun and practical outdoor fabric for loose-covered cushions.

For this dockside luncheon, the view is what counts, but a few simple touches make the open space an open-air room. Create your own ceiling – and protect yourself from the sun's harmful rays – with a wide garden umbrella. Box cushions set out on the dock add comfortable seating (many patio styles come in weatherproof fabrics). If you want to keep a side table or a couple of chairs outdoors through the season, choose pieces made of a weather-friendly wood like teak or cedar, or painted furniture like this pair of Adirondack chairs.

A dockside picnic, *left*, benefits from the cool shade of an umbrella. Wide arms on the Adirondack chairs make a lunch table unnecessary; one side can hold a plate, the other a cold drink. **Fruit salad**, *above*, served in ice cream cones propped in a metal basket, is as easy to eat as it is to carry. A beach towel makes the perfect waterside tablecloth.

How to Lay an Outdoor Table

Eating outdoors is always more appealing when the lighting is right, the setting is special, and everything you need is within easy reach. Whether you pack a picnic for a day at the beach, share supper on the veranda, or enjoy a snack by the pool, many of the best outdoor settings are also quietly restorative. Employ a few of the tricks shown here to eliminate forgotten items, help cut down on trips back to the kitchen, and add style to outdoor dining. Use handled containers to transport table basics; fasten whole place settings together with a simple clothes peg; and hang votives overhead to give the night sky a warm glow.

Lanterns containing flickering votives, *above*, hang at varying heights from a veranda ceiling to create the effect of an illuminated chandelier. You might also tie them to the lower limbs of a tree in the garden for a romantic candlelit dinner under the stars. **Glossy beach stones**, *right*, embellished with simple string, are charming decorative additions to a formal outdoor table, but they work hard, too: the smooth rocks keep the lightweight tablecloth in place when the wind picks up.

A **cutting board**, *left*, is a clever, portable place mat for a poolside snack. A folded napkin stands in as a plate, and a simple green leaf serves as a coaster for a refreshing drink. **Picnic place settings**, *below left*, are prepared for a windy day at the beach. Clothes pegs secure paper plates to sunny acrylic tumblers. **A galvanized container**, *below*, is set on an étagère and outfitted with veranda dining essentials. The bucket holds cutlery, condiments, and tealights, and it is easily carried from kitchen to table.

lighting

Whether rosy morning sunlight or deep evening shadows, the quality and quantity of light can change the atmosphere of a room completely. Since a dining room is used throughout the day, it's especially important to consider the mood that natural light creates here. Design for versatility, so that lighting is flexible and can be matched to the time of day or occasion – a soothing glow for evening meals, ample light for projects. Think of lighting as your furnishings' better half. It helps define colours, sets the mood, and dictates where the table sits best.

providing a blend of both. Finally, decide which objects or architectural features you might highlight with accent lighting. Create beautiful atmospheric patterns with candlelight. Whether pillars, votives, or a classic candelabra, candles can always be used in abundance. Don't be afraid to use multiples: cluster tealights for a casual event, arrange tapers for a more formal one.

When designing your lighting plan, be sure to factor in the ways that lamplight and natural daylight will interact. Both window treatments and lighting fixtures should be adjustable to work

The basics of dining room lighting are simple: indirect is always better than direct, lamps and candles should be positioned to flatter guests, and flexibility is key.

A dining room that must accommodate meals at various times of the day and entertaining for a range of occasions requires a versatile, layered lighting plan. There are three types of lighting: ambient, task, and accent. Begin with ambient, which gives a room an overall wash of light and gently illuminates everything in it. Its source can be anything from a single overhead fixture to a row of track lights set uniformly overhead.

Next, decide how you want to light the table. A mix of indirect lighting for dining and flexible task lighting for eating, cooking, and working is best. Easily focussed table lamps, pendant fixtures, or wall-mounted gallery lights do well by

in harmony with one another. Translucent sheers help prevent glare by softly filtering light throughout the day. Add a decorative curtain layer to cover the windows in the evening.

Think about small practicalities, too. The right match between lampshade and light bulb may be all that's needed to give your dining room an ideal wash of light. Incandescent, fluorescent, and halogen bulbs each have their own colours of illumination. The best way to find the right shade or bulb for a fixture is to experiment with different styles and wattages. Installing dimmers is a must – use them to enjoy all the variations that light and shadow have to offer.

Lighting for Entertaining

Whether set for a holiday celebration or a romantic dinner, a table dressed up with candlelight is a luxury that everyone can afford. Envelop your dining room in a soft overall glow accented with a row of flickering candles, and a fine party becomes unforgettable.

Adjustable lighting is as basic to the well-designed dining room as tables and chairs, and as important to entertaining as the guest list. When the plan calls for an evening event, start by creating a soft overall glow, then lavish the room in sparkling glass and the pure beauty of candlelight.

Combined with mirrors, silver, and a little overhead illumination to banish deep shadows, candlelight draws focus inwards and softens edges. An indispensable ingredient for a dinner party, candlelight highlights the faces of your guests. Aim for variety: cluster clear glass votives at the table's centre, and set an array of pierced ceramic holders on either side. Mix in single stems of tall white flowers, such as the orchids in this dining room, and their blooms will appear to float above the glow of the table.

Whether your dining room is large or small, lighting draws attention wherever it is focussed. A mirror set at one end of the room reflects light warmly throughout the evening hours. Here, a mirrored buffet set with sparkling decanters shines as brilliantly as a fireplace hearth.

A vintage clock face, *left*, with a silvered back is used as a glittering tray, reflecting the flicker of tealights. **Low votives around a mirrored centrepiece**, *right*, set a romantic mood and encourage conversation. Place settings suggest the play of light and shadow with matt black ceramic condiment bowls set on top of simple, wide-rimmed white china.

When you're setting a stage for entertaining, plan the lighting to bring out the important elements. Use light to draw attention to displayed objects, create patterns, and reveal interesting textures. Gradations of light give a room greater depth, which is appealing and romantic. As night falls, the drama of the lighting emerges.

Glass decanters, *above*, shine when lit by recessed lights in a Victorian dresser. The mirrored cupboard gently reflects the shimmer of glassware on the table, creating a glow at eye-level for seated guests. **Light and dark achieve high contrast**, *right*, with trim white drum shades, layered table linen, dinner plates, and orchids all balancing the dark walls. The simple furnishings work well for family dining, or they can be dressed up with accessories and a variety of lighting for more festive events.

Design Details

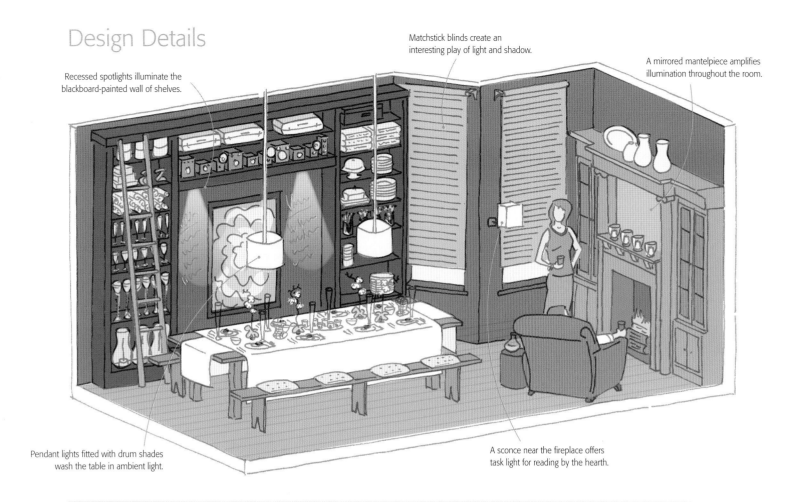

Recessed spotlights illuminate the blackboard-painted wall of shelves.

Matchstick blinds create an interesting play of light and shadow.

A mirrored mantelpiece amplifies illumination throughout the room.

Pendant lights fitted with drum shades wash the table in ambient light.

A sconce near the fireplace offers task light for reading by the hearth.

Colour Palette

A restrained composition of black and white underscores the drama that lighting creates. The palette plays with light and shadow, from the white drum shades and the china arranged on the black bookshelves to the white chalk against the blackboard. By candlelight, the wood floors and trim acquire a warm glow. The dark wall appears to recede, allowing the animation of faces around the luminous table to be the centrepiece of any evening.

Room Plan

Thoroughly considered lighting, floor-to-ceiling shelves, and simple furnishings work together to make this room the perfect space for all manner of gatherings, from a family dinner to an elegant dinner party. The room offers adjustable lighting options, including dimmers for the overhead light, sconce, and display lights. The wall of black shelves gets an extra wash of light from recessed spotlights over the blackboard. A sconce light is placed by the fireplace for reading. Mirrors at both ends of the room make the space seem larger than it might otherwise.

Materials

Crystal A percentage of lead oxide in its formula gives crystal more sparkle than glass. Crystal is also softer, making it easier to cut and more refractive than glass.

Mirror Once made of glass backed with mercury and tin, mirrors are now back-coated with a silvering solution that creates a reflective surface.

Pine A softwood that ages to a golden patina, pine is highly regarded for its natural beauty and rich variations of honey colour.

Filtering Summer Light

With a few panels of voile and a table dressed up with some natural accents, you can bring the comfortable elegance of an indoor dining room out into the fresh air of a veranda.

Surprise your guests with a warm-weather dining room decorated with refined details. Start with sheer curtains that welcome the generous flow of sunlight. Add a handful of garden flowers arranged in a bouquet of small vases, and cushion each seat luxuriously. If you have something as elegant as this colourful shawl, you just might want to drape the table with it, for all to enjoy.

A study in contrast, *far left*, this veranda dining room sets a vintage wicker table with an antique shawl. **An ornamental birdcage**, *left*, is modified for use as a serving station. **Voile curtains**, *above*, are tied back with napkin rings.

A trio of striped votives, *below*, line up along a mirrored mantelpiece. Take cues from old-fashioned candle holders, which were made with a light reflector to double the glow of the flame, and arrange candles in front of a mirror. **Finds from nature**, *right*, can be attractive accents for pillar candles inside a hurricane glass. Partially fill an oversize candle holder with all manner of natural decorations. Consider fresh flowers and leaves, shells, stones, and beach glass. Avoid anything that's flammable, and, for candles other than tealights, always use a container that is designed to hold a candle.

How to Decorate with Candles

Candles shouldn't be saved for special occasions. Use them every day to give the dining room an animated glow. Whether clustered as a centrepiece or sprinkled throughout a room, a thoughtful candle arrangement marries style with practicality while instantly making a dining space feel festive. Votives (the unscented kind) or tealights (which come in little metal cups) are the most versatile options since they can be safely and easily tucked into a host of decorative containers. To create a unique tablescape, arrange votives in clusters combined with seasonal botanicals, or file tealights in a long line down the centre of a table.

A row of teacups, *left*, makes a pretty column down the centre of a table, each cup's delicate porcelain illuminated from within by a single tealight. Shasta daisies decorate each saucer, giving this simple lighting idea a finished look. **Fragrant coffee beans**, *above*, fill a trifle bowl and provide a sturdy and aromatic bed for tealights. The sheen of the coffee beans glimmers in the candlelight, creating a multi-sensory centrepiece. The glass bowl would be just as lovely filled with berries, hazelnuts, or glistening sweets.

Find Your Style A select guide to choosing and using the best

Ambient Lighting

Your dining room's ambient lighting provides an overall wash of light to illuminate the space and, most important, the table. By day, ambient light may be a combination of natural and artificial light. At night, it should give the room a diffused atmospheric radiance. The classic choice here is one overhead light source situated above the dining room table. Such fixtures are best fitted with incandescent bulbs, which give a warm light and attractively illuminate colours. Dimmers help moderate light levels for different times and occasions.

Downlight

Task Lighting

Task lighting is the concentrated light that helps you work in the kitchen and use your dining room table for various activities other than eating. Introduce it in these rooms through smaller, location-specific fixtures that direct a focussed pool of light. Most dining rooms and kitchens benefit from task lighting on work surfaces, on a bar area, and over a sideboard. When planning task lighting, aim for relatively close proximity to the area where it's needed, and consider the material and colour of the lampshade, both of which affect the efficacy of the light.

Sconces

Accent Lighting

Accent lighting creates mood and drama in the dining room with gentle strokes of light that can be moved around easily. More decorative than utilitarian, accent lighting is typically low level, so that it bounces flattering luminosity off surfaces rather than emitting a direct beam. Often, the lights themselves are beautiful accessories. Use accent lighting to draw attention to photos, collections, or displays. In the dining room, candlelight is the definitive accent light. Use pillars, tapers, or votives on the table and beyond to fill the room with a warm glow.

Votives

ambient, task, and accent lighting for your dining room

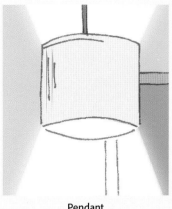

Pendant

Chandelier

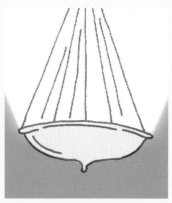

Suspended uplight

Downlights cast wide pools of light beneath them. They are great fixtures for over tables.

Pendants direct light both upwards and down. Their size and lining affect the breadth and colour of the light.

Chandeliers make a dramatic statement. Dimmers allow you to adjust the light levels.

Suspended uplights are ceiling-mounted fixtures that provide soft, glare-free illumination.

Suspended task lights

Under-cupboard lights

Gallery lights

Sconces are space-saving, wall-mounted fixtures that can cast light up, down, or sideways.

Suspended task lights hang directly over a work surface. Opaque shades help focus light.

Under-cupboard lights are usually recessed halogens. They offer good light for reading recipes or making coffee.

Gallery lights cast pools of light onto artwork or objects and can be positioned to minimize glare.

Display lights

Candles

Lanterns

Votives are candles in holders that prevent wax from dripping and offer a soft, decorative glow.

Display lights create glittering effects inside dressers and glass-fronted furnishings.

Candles create a warm and dramatic atmosphere by casting a golden light on a table top.

Lanterns shade bare bulbs from view and set against the backdrop of the night sky are festive for evening entertaining.

storage

In an ideal world, there is a place for everything and everything has its place. While this maxim may seem out of touch with the way you really live, you don't necessarily need to be a minimalist to break free of clutter. In fact, getting organized is easier than you might think. Order simply begins with good storage, and it actually helps if you have a well-stocked dining room.

How do you usually use your dining room? Before adding more storage, explore your family's range of everyday activities. If you eat all your meals at the dining room table and

For a swept-clean look, put some storage undercover. In a dining room, sideboards are especially suited to help bridge the gap from open to closed storage. They let you keep favourite pieces at hand and stow the rest in closed compartments. Many corner cupboards and dressers also mix open display space with enclosed storage.

In a small space, wall-hung cupboards keep items off worktops and table tops. With the doors off or paned with glass, you can appreciate and view their contents. In larger spaces, storage options are plentiful, but so are the potential dining areas

In a dining room, organization can create real beauty. A row of glassware, a stack of plates – simple things that are neatly arranged become lovely decorations.

gather there for holidays and celebrations, too, you'll want everyday dishes and tableware at your fingertips, along with fine china and table linen stored nearby. If your dining area is part of an open kitchen, cooking projects are likely to spill over into the space, so you'll want those supplies easily accessible. If it's used primarily for special occasions, then the dining room is the perfect spot to house fine china or a silver collection.

Open storage is especially appealing because so many dining necessities have beautiful shapes. If you like having everything in view, open shelves can be artfully arranged. Built-in cupboards can be customized to fit unusual serving pieces.

in the room – consider movable storage that easily transports wherever you need it. Movable storage can be practically anything: beautiful bowls, woven boxes, glass vessels. Cutlery can be kept in a wide-mouth vase or shallow basket.

Consider the whole room and the things you need to have in it, and then decide what type of system suits your requirements and your style. Storage must be functional, but it never has to be boring. Look for unusual storage solutions and allow some room to experiment. Storage that's both useful and decorative is important to every room, especially this one, because you just never know when company may be calling.

Storage for an Open-Plan Kitchen

A welcoming kitchen is where real life takes place, making it the hardest-working – and most frequented – space in the house. Storage at every level, a versatile layout, and a little creativity are all it takes to make this favourite destination a place to stop and stay awhile.

The simple pleasures of eating and entertaining make eat-in kitchens one of the most popular spaces in the house. Kitchens are "family central", especially when they open onto a dining area. They require careful storage planning that combines the functions of the space – meal preparation, eating, entertaining – with all the little flourishes that make a kitchen-dining area a place where you'll want to linger.

The secret to a classic integrated eating space is dedicating some storage to each specific function. If you look closely, you'll notice that the storage allows this spacious kitchen to accommodate many activities at the same time and still maintain a calm atmosphere. Laid out with efficient and organized cooking areas, the broken-U arrangement helps make meals for two or entertaining twenty equally effortless.

A generous island, deep and high enough to be used as a kitchen table, is the focal point and favourite gathering place in this kitchen. The china cupboard is positioned near the sink, making clearing up easy and efficient. The stacked dishwashers, which store dishes as well as clean them, make the most of the little space they occupy. A wine storage unit and desk are built in along the pathway to the dining room, taking full advantage of the interior wall.

Glazed earthenware bowls, *left*, make decorative and movable storage for pantry items and table linen. **The deep island**, *right*, offers drawers for cutlery at waist height and a shelf for oversize serving pieces below.

The key to keeping this room organized lies in three types of storage: built-in, movable, and open storage that doubles as display. Drawers are sized to suit the items they hold to avoid needless rummaging. Shallow drawers are for cutlery and spices, deep ones for pots and pans. Built-in glass-front cupboards hold everyday dishes that are attractive enough to display, while panelled versions keep utilitarian and less frequently used cookware out of sight. A low shelf in the island holds large, heavy items. An open shelf over the cooker is both functional and decorative, especially when filled with a collection of olive oils.

A bright window sill, *above*, functions as storage and display for an artistic arrangement of red bitters. **Comfortable saddle seat stools**, *right*, slide under the island, clearing the pathway to the dining room. The sink and drawer-style dishwasher are positioned behind a wall that was made tall enough to hide them from the view of guests in the dining room.

From the dining room side of an open-plan space, the dividing wall or return worktop should be high enough to hide kitchen work surfaces. Keep things looking neat and trim by limiting open storage to the kitchen area. Place furniture or plan built-in cupboards along the dining area walls that are away from the flow of traffic. Concealed storage offers a secure place to store china and serving pieces out of sight but close at hand. Here, a long, low shelf on top of the built-in storage unit doubles as a sideboard and a display area for artwork at the ideal viewing level for those seated at the table.

A low wall of built-in storage, *left*, in the dining area is designed for style and function with alternating drawers and cupboards custom-fit for cutlery, table linen, and trays. **Table-ready place settings**, *above*, kept conveniently in deep baskets on the sideboard, await a meal for two or ten.

Design Details

Unloading the dishwasher is easy when dishes are stored nearby.

Built-in cupboards double as a sideboard and storage space.

A bulky refrigerator vanishes from view when set into a recessed space.

A panelled return partially separates the kitchen from the dining area.

The room's open layout offers both formal and casual dining areas.

Colour Palette

A range of yellows and greens – from pale gold to sage – and white are the essence of this kitchen-dining room's palette. Accents such as the glazed pottery and surface materials like the wood floor are interesting variations of yellow, while the marble worktop adds subtle depth to the lighter side of the palette. Green accessories, such as table linen and potted plants, indicate the transition from kitchen to dining room.

Room Plan

This kitchen-dining room has storage space at every level, and the broken-U arrangement keeps movement between the two areas effortless. Open shelving acts as storage and as display for wine glasses and cookery books. The island, which doubles as a casual dining surface, hides a shelf where mixing bowls and pantry supplies slot neatly out of sight. The cooker features shelves for storing utensils and ingredients. The path to the dining room is free of clutter, with the island stools and desk seating designed to be tucked away to keep traffic flowing freely.

Materials

Stainless steel Hard-wearing and hygienic, stainless steel is impervious to food acids and can handle the heat of pots and pans.

Panelling This decorative wall lining introduces a warm wood element to the coolness of standard kitchen materials, like stainless steel, ceramic, and marble.

Marble Polished marble has a glossy surface that reflects light and emphasizes the beauty of this material's natural colour and markings.

Storage with Style

Setting out your favourite china to be admired is a clever and easy way to bring special interest to a dining room. Storage made visible keeps the decorative possibilities open. This wall of shelves offers lessons in storage and display that any well-stocked dining room would be wise to follow.

Storing glassware, tableware, or a bar behind closed doors may be traditional, but a closer look at the simple beauty of dinnerware, silver bar paraphernalia, and freshly folded table linen suggests it should be otherwise. Setting out your dining room wares instead of packing them away is a smart approach that addresses storage and style at the same time. You might start by rethinking the location of the dining area itself. Shake things up by moving the dining table to any space that offers shelving – a library, perhaps, or part of an open-plan living room. If changing rooms is too much, make a smaller change and replace an existing sideboard or dresser with floor-to-ceiling shelves. This display approach to storage offers benefits besides good looks: it puts everything out where you can see it so you save time spent searching for it. It also reminds you to use special tableware more often, adding variety to everyday meals.

If you dream of a pulled-together look, arrange shelves for practicality first. Providing for the way tableware really gets used makes laying the table easier and increases the likelihood that things will be returned to their proper place.

Aperitifs look inviting, *left*, staged on top of a lacquered built-in drinks cabinet. Arrange attractive liquor bottles and glasses in logical order for mixing drinks. **Store place settings together**, *right*, to lay the table in fewer steps. Stacked plates and cutlery add an enticing china-shop quality to the shelf.

This dramatic loft dining space benefits from a series of brick arches that naturally divide the storage wall into equal sections. In each, storage takes a gallery approach, but also shows off the art of caring for all the provisions of the table. Everyday dishes, glassware, table linen, and other essentials are on the accessible lower tiers, with better wine glasses, china, and cookery books above them. On top shelves, cherished fragile pieces mingle with collectables. In the lowest tier, fine wines and fine linen are protected from light. Wine bottles with corks should always be stored on their sides to keep the corks moist.

Gilt-rimmed china, *above*, is pretty even when stored properly, with acid-free paper or felt liners between each piece to protect against chips and cracks. **Paisley throws**, *right*, instead of a conventional cloth, make an elegant table covering. An ironstone soup tureen stands in for a vase.

Design Details

Colour Palette

If you live in a large or loft-like space, bold colours are a good choice because they create a sense of enclosure. Earth-toned brick red and burgundy, in particular, are warming and inviting, and can create low-key elegance when used as the room's primary colours. In this loft, the colours in the exposed brick wall naturally suggest a play between dark red and grey. The brick mortar acts as a median colour between deep reds and white china. Neutral linen loose covers repeat the same tone.

Fragile table linen is rolled, unstarched, in acid-free tissue to avoid discolouration. Everyday place mats and napkins are tied with ribbon in tidy bundles. With so many items on view, the dining area becomes an opportunity to combine your collections in new, creative ways. Vary your serving pieces, glassware, plates, and bowls. Mix patterns or pair vintage china with modern for a bold, stylish look. Add flair by placing table decorations off-centre, leaving space open for guests to converse easily and pass or pour the wine. Here, slender candlesticks anchor one end of the table, and a generous tureen filled with flowers completes the tableau at the other end.

Rolled inside a metallic puzzle ring, *left*, a cherry red napkin rests on a bright white soup bowl to emphasize its colour. **Fine table linen**, *above*, is laid flat, wrapped with acid-free paper, and then rolled rather than folded to prevent mould or permanent creases. Each one is tied with a grosgrain ribbon for handsome display on open shelves.

Materials

Brick Old exposed brick gives a room immediate history. Architectural brick appears mostly in shades of red and brown, while glazed brick, like ceramic tile, comes in countless colours. Bricks laid in intricate perpendicular patterns can create added visual and textural interest.

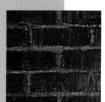

Paisley Typically made of soft wool woven into an intricately patterned shawl, paisley is synonymous with the tadpole-shaped motif of textiles originating in India. Taking its name from the Scottish mill town where these shawls were reproduced, paisley makes a warm, stylish statement.

Gilt-edged china Formal dinnerware embellished with real gold, platinum, or silver accents requires special treatment. Never use it in a microwave, and use care when storing, washing, and handling to prevent the gilding from rubbing off.

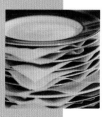
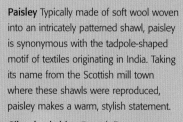

A glass tumbler, *top*, is a useful container for napkins and cutlery, and can be easily carried from cupboard to table. Woven bowls, *above*, are stacked on their corresponding dinner plates, a logical storage arrangement when it's time to lay the table. A collection of creamware, *right*, demonstrates a simple storage trick. If your dining room has open storage, create subtle organization by keeping the display all the same colour.

How to Organize Tableware

When you know exactly where your dishes, table linen, and cutlery are located and can access them easily, laying the table is a simple task. If you're lucky enough to have a grand space, it's wise to organize with an eye towards convenience; you don't want to be carrying plates and glasses right across the room. In a small room, assemble your dining necessities artfully and logically to help save space. For glass-fronted or open shelves, keep things neat by placing like items – similar in style, colour, or material – on the same shelf. Collect small items, like napkin rings and coasters, in attractive containers such as woven baskets or glass canisters.

Generous open shelving, *left*, is more than a place to stow your goods; with a little creative arranging, it's a place to show them off as well. Multiples of anything make storage shelves look more organized – lots of glasses on one shelf, for example, and lots of plates on the next. Here, bottles of champagne (wrapped in tissue paper to keep out damaging light) are kept handy for pouring, just above the champagne glasses.
Matching glass canisters, *above*, borrow an idea from shop displays and keep napkin rings and table linen sorted, visible, and neatly organized.

display

Celebrate the things you love by displaying them for all to see. When thoughtfully arranged, just about any possession, object, keepsake, or find from nature can inspire our thoughts, lift our spirits, remind us of a certain time or place, or simply invite a smile.

The dining room is an especially rich source of objects that are inherently beautiful and deserve pride of place: polished silver, a collection of table linen, pretty plates, delicate crystal and glass, and textured pottery. From the simplest set of white bowls to priceless porcelain, tableware encouraging guests to linger and enjoy their surroundings. In the dining room, use display to reinforce a sense of order as well as to enhance the decor. Repetition is a display trick you can employ for anything from storing glassware to hanging framed art. Items of similar colours always look good together, even when they differ in style and shape. Consider pottery, porcelain, and glass, for example. Alternatively, a diverse collection of similar items – whether candles or corkscrews – can be presented as a group to unify the differences among them. A single material can

The things we use every day are the most important: dinnerware, table linen, glassware, and cutlery. Display makes art of the objects that please us most.

instantly becomes a sculptural element when set out on a sideboard or placed on an illuminated shelf in a china cupboard. Artfully arranged, even the most basic dining implements can be enjoyed as display, whether it's fine silverware stored in a glass tumbler or a row of vases on a window ledge. In fact, in a small dining space or one with open shelves, tableware can be the primary – and most stunning – decoration. The trick is all in the placement, so that dining room essentials look beautiful but are also within easy reach.

Of course, displays needn't be limited to items you use every day. Collections, photos, family heirlooms, and framed artwork all have a role in make a dramatic display, such as hotel silver displayed on a shelf. When arranging objects, stagger rows in both height and depth for a sense of rhythm, or set out three or five things in a group (odd numbers are pleasantly asymmetrical).

Whether you decide to create a whole display wall or simply set a few pictures on the mantel, keep in mind that in the dining room most of our time is spent sitting at the table. This gives you the freedom to place favourite objects a little lower than you might in other rooms. It also creates a primary focal point in the centre of the table where a changing seasonal display is a nice way to surprise guests and keep the room feeling fresh.

Creating a Dining Room Gallery

When it's also a home for cherished collections, a dining room can be far more than a place to enjoy food. Favourite objects extend a sense of welcome as soon as you walk into the room. Present the things you love in a beautiful way, and your home will be beautiful, too.

Think of the dining room as your own personal gallery, a place where the display reflects you, your family, and the season. Start with a neutral backdrop and use it as a canvas on which to express your inspirations and memories. All-white walls and ceilings, which are often favoured by art galleries, recede into the background and help highlight displays of all kinds. If white is too spare for your tastes, think monochromatic. Walls with a peach or yellow tint accentuate the warm tones in many wooden objects; those with a hint of cool lavender enhance all types of silver metal.

Displays don't need to be large or valuable to be fascinating. Photographs of any size, children's artwork, or even swatches of a favourite fabric gain presence when they're set in an interesting frame. If photos are what you love, you can display them on just about any size wall or on any amount of shelf space. Or, you can carry one theme across several stages, as in this spare dining space devoted to all things botanical. Along with beautifully framed photographs, an enlargement of a leaf detail, printed at the local copying shop and protected by Perspex, acts as a graphic table covering. Use the same technique to display a collection of images, so that your "tablecloth" can be changed according to season or occasion.

Finds from nature, *left*, lend a narrative to an all-white table setting. An aspen leaf motif embellishes a napkin at each place setting. **Fig branches in a clear vase**, *right*, are as artfully arranged as the pictures on the walls.

A collection of black-and-white photographs establishes the elegant scheme of this room. Framed gallery-style, with wide mounts surrounding small images, the photographs hang about 1.5 m (5 ft) from the floor for optimum viewing. A symmetrical arrangement on the wall, with each picture hung equidistant from the next, creates an atmosphere that's soothing and serene. Planning such a layout is easy. Cut out frame-size pieces of kraft paper and arrange them on the walls before hanging your pictures.

A mix of hotel silver serving pieces, *left*, is kept at hand for easy access and arranged to create a striking display. Gravy boats, wine chillers, chargers, and platters attract attention in beautiful still-life arrangements. **Beaded wine-glass charms**, *above*, shaped like bunches of grapes, are suspended by ribbons from the branches of the centrepiece.

Collectors choose furniture for displaying their wares as meticulously as they do the treasured pieces themselves. However, a simple table or bookcase can serve just as well as a china cupboard, provided it has clean lines and a pleasing shape. Here, a low line of office bookcases sits at just the right height for diners to enjoy the view into each compartment. The dark background inside each shelf produces a shadow-box effect that places the silver objects in high relief. Each piece of crystal, old and new silver, and white china on display is a memento of special occasions and a reminder of celebrations yet to come.

Glass cylinder vases, *left*, introduce a splash of colour and a modern take on the traditional floral arrangement, with pink roses floating at various depths. Below, open shelves are roomy enough for tall wine buckets and wide tureens. **Antique silver ladles**, *above*, rest in an heirloom vegetable dish, polished by generations of users.

Design Details

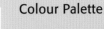

Colour Palette

White, deep brown, and silver compose a sophisticated colour palette in this collector's dining room. White-on-white walls and mouldings provide a perfect gallery backdrop for any collection. Here, they emphasize and define the photography and objects on display for a clean, contemporary look. Against the white walls, dark frames and bookcases stand out, drawing attention to their contents. The espresso-coloured table and chairs have warm undertones, which create an intriguing contrast to the cool silver collection.

Materials

Stained wood Unlike painted finishes, stained wood has a rich, but translucent, depth of colour that allows the grain to show through. Available in many shades, the lustre of stained wood adds both visual and physical texture to a space.

Coin silver Because of material shortages, many silver objects made before 1860 were created from melted silver coins. A slightly less pure alloy than sterling silver, coin silver has become collectable, partly due to its warm tones.

Silver A prized material for centuries, silver comes in many forms: pure silver, coin silver, sterling silver, and silver plate, each with slight variations in colour. Old hotel silver is especially collectable. Made with silver-plated nickel, it is heavier than other types of silver, which made it ideal for use as serving pieces on luxury ocean liners.

A Collector's Kitchen

An eat-in kitchen has a charm all its own. Here, the combined pleasures of cooking and dining come together to create an intimate place for easy conversations with the cook. Display collections and treasures high and low to personalize the surroundings with whimsy and delight.

Great cooks are often great collectors, lovingly amassing culinary stockpiles and vintage kitchen finds. Eating in a collector's kitchen can be something like going to the theatre. There's always some kind of performance under way, whether it's the music of clanging pots and pans or the quieter assembly of a collector's passions in pretty tableaux on the walls, shelves, worktops, or table. Often, the kitchen is the best place to put special treasures to use. It's where a set of mixing bowls can double as an artful display, and where teacups can invite pleasant mealtime reveries.

From a weathered antique milk jug to a sleek new stainless steel appliance, objects displayed in an eat-in kitchen enjoy pride of place, because so much time is spent looking at them. In fact, it may be the best place in the house for displaying your favourite collections. A passion for recycling, reclaiming, and reusing is the evident theme in this Arts and Crafts kitchen. Collectables populate every surface, creating a topography of interests and souvenirs, culinary and otherwise. The simplicity of this all-wood kitchen offers a perfect background to the display, though any warm, neutral palette would create the same effect.

A rustic kitchen, *left*, was built (in the true spirit of a collector) from wood salvaged during the refurbishment of this cottage. **Salt and pepper shakers from the 1940s**, *right*, oversee a collection of vintage glassware put to use on a rough-hewn lazy Susan crafted from a wine barrel lid.

Every surface in a kitchen is a potential space to display collections, from the deep worktops to the tops of wall cupboards. A display can tell a story or be purely decorative. The most attractive displays are made up of treasures linked by a similar theme, colour, or texture. Here, collections are arranged with the skill of a set designer. Old-fashioned pickling jars become unexpected decorations placed high above the cupboard. A basket filled with wooden rolling pins marks the end of a long bench. Quirky groupings and intriguing vignettes add interest throughout the room.

Accents of grass green, *above*, both old and new, tie together collectables ranging from green pottery to garden urns, in this wood-panelled kitchen. A miniature horse-drawn cart doubles as centrepiece and holder for salt and pepper shakers. **A floor-to-ceiling display of collections**, *right*, holds something of interest at all levels and makes use of every inch of space. Pickling jars and ironstone jugs are arranged up high, vintage apothecary glass and weathered baskets down below. Muted rugs enjoy a new life as upholstery, folded and draped over the kitchen benches to soften seating.

Design Details

Colour Palette

If you have collections to display, a tonal palette (a set of colours that share an underlying hue) is a wise choice. The similarity in hues will keep the collection looking neatly unified, while the differences will introduce a pleasing, subtle variety. The mix of items in this kitchen is a good example, showing the brightest greens in the table linen and pottery, greyer greens in the overhead light fixtures and garden urn. The rest of the palette is made up of neutrals – grey, brown, and white – which place the green in the foreground and nicely complement the patina of the kitchen's timeworn treasures.

Materials

American art pottery Highly collectable, these decorative pieces were produced from the early 1900s to the 1940s, in a range of glazes, patterns, and shapes that reflect the Art Deco, Art Nouveau, and Prairie Style movements of the period.

Fir If you want a rustic look, the characteristics of scrubbed fir are what you're after. This softwood ages quickly and beautifully, making it especially appealing in restorations or older homes.

Salvaged wood The rough finish of recycled wood gives a room history and warmth with its distinct grain and wear. Salvaged wood gains extra character with nicks and dents, and is a counterpoint to glass or metal kitchen appliances. Salvaged wood is often available in larger planks than newly milled timber.

A mixed collection of green pottery and cut branches brings the beauty of an outside garden to a window seat. Combined with pieces of laboratory glass, which are used to showcase the finest specimens from the garden, the collection is married by colour. This simple grouping relies on a few display basics to create a visually powerful study in balance and scale. Larger vases descend to smaller bowls in the centre of the display. A staggered arrangement of pottery in odd numbers is interspersed with clear glass pieces to create an asymmetry that's pleasing to the eye.

Matt green art pottery, *left*, from the 1920s and '30s creates a harmonious tone-on-tone colour study, though shapes and sizes vary dramatically. Mixed with sleek laboratory glass, pieces are arranged to play up their different textures and silhouettes. **Lightweight window blinds**, *above*, suspended by a simple bamboo rod, roll up or down to provide a sunny exposure.

How to Arrange Floral Centrepieces

They're meant to lend a decorative note to a dinner table, but centrepieces can also showcase your flair with flowers. Nothing dictates the mood of a gathering – formal, simple, romantic, or playful – like the flowers you choose and the way you arrange them on a table. Almost any presentation will work if you give it your own personal touch. From a humble tin to a proud crystal vase, the options are only as limited as your imagination. Once you've found the right vessel, arrange flowers in a simple shape and set them on your table. Have fun: opt for dramatic oversize vases or a single bud vase for each place setting.

A crystal vodka chiller, *above,* is reinvented as a sparkling centrepiece when shot glasses are filled with delicate blossoms of scarlet lantana. **Recycled tomato tins,** *right,* make graphically pleasing containers for bouquets of fresh tulips and Queen Anne's lace. They are arranged in a row down the centre of a banquet table for a casual gathering. To support loose bunches, set juice glasses or smaller vases inside the cans. **A dramatic blown-glass vase,** *opposite,* is the ideal frame for a generous cluster of roses in full bloom, each one cut to reach the globe-shaped centre of the vase. You can use any clear glass container to achieve this still-life effect by simply filling it part way with water and trimming the roses down to fit inside.

Room Resources

We believe that casual style is something you can weave through every space in your home, from front rooms to private havens. For this book, we scoured hundreds of locations to find perfect settings to create rooms just for you. We experimented with dining tables and chairs, linen, rugs, curtains, tableware, and accessories to find the best combinations for each space. The results? This collection of style ideas, which we hope will inspire and delight you.

Each location chosen for this book was unique and interesting. Here is a little bit more about each of the homes we visited, the style ideas we created, and the individual elements that make each design tick.

A note about colour: wherever it was possible in this list of resources, we've offered the actual paint manufacturer and paint colour that was used in the room shown. We also list the closest Benjamin Moore paint colour match (in parentheses). Because photography and colour printing processes can dramatically change the way colours appear, it is very important to test swatches of any paint colour you are considering in your own home, where you can see how the light affects them at different times of the day.

Easy Elegance for Everyday Dining

Located on the ground floor of a gracious Victorian townhouse, this dining room has formal front windows with original mouldings.

Space The dining room is located in what was originally the living room of the house. Its high ceilings, ornate mantel, and tall windows are common features of Victorian architecture. The floors are narrow-board oak.

Colour Walls (Benjamin Moore Butter 2023-60, flat). Trim (Benjamin Moore Lemon Ice OC-114, satin).

Furnishings Platinum dining table, Megan chairs, velvet slipcovers, Hem-stitch table runner and napkins, Great White dinnerware, Spiegelau wine glasses, Roma barware, hammered cutlery, Great Wine decanters, modular wine bar, paisley rug, ice bucket, and Voluminous vases and candlesticks, all from Pottery Barn.

Lighting Five-arm brass chandelier.

Display Canvases painted with Benjamin Moore colours: Greenbrier Beige HC-79, Bleeker Beige HC-80, Manchester Tan HC-81, Mesa Verde Tan HC-76, Pismo Dunes AC-32, Hot Spring Stones AC-31, Davenport Tan HC-76, Alexandria Beige HC-77, Litchfield Gray HC-78.

pages 14–21

Creating a Banquet

Designed by California architect John Marsh Davis, this house is set amid groves of pine and madrona trees. Exposed beams throughout the house are salvaged redwood.

Space Built by James Lino Construction, the house features custom-built walnut bookcases and built-in storage. Both the great room and den feature Rumford fireplaces designed to reflect heat into the large, high-ceilinged rooms.

Colour Walls (Benjamin Moore Hawthorne Yellow HC-4, satin).

Furnishings Gustavian chairs in mahogany, Great White dinnerware, Classic cutlery, Burton sofa in oat Everyday Suede, Manhattan recliner in caramel, Melange Gabbeh rug, Henry occasional table, acrylic bowls, Ashland coffee table, and chenille throw, all from Pottery Barn. Vino Grande white wine glasses and balloon stems from Williams-Sonoma. Chocolate jacquard weave linen napkins, paprika linen fabric, Murano glass cherries from Swallowtail, San Francisco.

Lighting Pillar candles from Pottery Barn. Stem lamps and Isabel lampshades by Nima Oberoi for Lunares, San Francisco.

Display Personalized frame from Pottery Barn. Photograph by Gina Risso, Gina Risso Photography, GinaRisso.com.

pages 30–39

Hosting a Casual Buffet

This open-plan house, designed by architect John Marsh Davis, overlooks a tidal waterway. Inside, the doors and fireplace mantel are made of 14-year-old curly redwood.

Space The house is 195 sq m (2,100 sq ft) and shares the property with a guest house and carpentry workshop. Much of the interior is built of reclaimed wood milled by the homeowner. All doors and trim are made of salvaged bridge timber.

Colour Walls Kelly Moore Pompeiian Red, flat (Benjamin Moore Iron Ore Red 2089-10).

Furnishings Meyer dining chairs, Sausalito dinnerware in blanca, Arctic cutlery, Luna salad servers, Great White soup tureen, Burton sofa, Manhattan leather chair, Melange chenille throw and cushions in cornflower, Checkerboard rug, Bosphorous cylinder vase, Hapao stacking wine rack, and Savannah basket, all from Pottery Barn. Breadboard and bread knife from Williams-Sonoma. Custom-built casework by James Lino.

Lighting Berkeley Floor lamp and iron rope chandelier with square linen shades from Pottery Barn.

Display Stone bowl by Michael Barnett. Painting *Untitled: White and gray*, acrylic and oil on canvas by Peter J. Ismert.

pages 47–53

Making the Most of a Small Space

Set on a quiet waterfront street, this 1912 Georgian-style, steel and brick building was originally built as a foreign consulate.

Space The renovated house features a delicate balance of rough and smooth surfaces, and old and new finishes, throughout. The dining alcove is part of an eat-in kitchen that juxtaposes the exposed brick walls of the original structure with state-of-the-art appliances. Architectural renovation by BRU Architects, San Francisco.

Furnishings Francisco table, Schoolhouse chairs, Great White dinnerware, soup tureen, and cake stand, Arctic cutlery, and Classic stemware, all from Pottery Barn. Assorted wine decanters, white table linen, and mixing bowls from Williams-Sonoma. Assorted stemware from Prize, San Francisco.

Display Clip display by etcbangkok.com.

pages 54–59

Setting for the Season

Located in a hilltop neighbourhood, high above the street, this mid-twentieth century Monterey-style house has a narrow front veranda that overlooks a busy shipping harbour.

Space The traditional style of this home works well with the antique and vintage furnishings found throughout the space. The dining room is just off the hallway, and connects to a modern kitchen through a discreet swinging door.

Colour Walls (Benjamin Moore Amber Waves 2159-40, flat).

Furnishings Bordeaux table, French country chairs, Hemstitch tablecloth, Sausalito dinnerware in amber, natural, and blanca, hammered cutlery, Soire glassware in amber, Springwood charger, Great White cake stands, silk organza curtains, bronzed component rod with turned glass finials, and Sundari kilim rug, all from Pottery Barn. Carolina table and chairs from Pottery Barn Kids. Table runner and napkins from The Gardener, Berkeley, California. Ironstone urns and platters from Prize, San Francisco. Other ironstone from Columbine, Corte Madera, California.

Lighting Pillar candles from Pottery Barn.

pages 66–71

Mixing Old and New

Steps from the street, this two-storey shingled cottage hides behind tall hedges. The front porch overlooks a cottage garden edged with flowering borders and roses.

Space In the open-plan living area, the modern kitchen shares space with a den alcove and a rustically decorated dining area. Floors are knotty pine stained in walnut, worktops are stone. The oven is by Thermador.

Colour Walls (Benjamin Moore Fernwood Green 2145-40, flat). Trim (Benjamin Moore Snowfall White 2144-70, satin).

Furnishings Haley bench, Schoolhouse armchairs and breakfast bar chairs, Dana bowls, hammered cutlery, oval wire baskets, and Colorbound sisal rug, all from Pottery Barn. Verre glasses from Williams-Sonoma. Woven bowls from Tail of the Yak, Berkeley, California. Twine place mats from Papaya, Sydney, Australia. Vintage table linen from Lacis, Berkeley, California. Napkins from Sue Fisher King, San Francisco. Green swirl glasses from Prize, San Francisco. Royal Sketches green transferware tureen from Swallowtail, San Francisco. Spotted and striped china by Terramoto Ceramics.

Lighting Fisherman's lights from Pottery Barn.

pages 82–89

Versatile Dining Room Classics

Home to an architect and an interior designer, this hillside estate has a guest house and pool house and is sited towards vineyard views.

Space The modern kitchen-dining area has dual sinks, one for food prep, one for cooking. A baking centre is located at the far end. To keep the kitchen airy and open, there are no overhead cupboards and all appliances are hidden.

Colour Walls and ceilings Fuller O'Brien White Wing, flat, (Benjamin Moore White Heron OC-57).

Furnishings Napoleon chairs, Schoolhouse bar stools, Great White dinnerware, Sausalito dinnerware in merlot, Great Wine glasses, pewter cutlery, Seagrass chair and ottoman, and block print cushions, all from Pottery Barn. Tea towels, terracotta bowls, and bread baskets all from Williams-Sonoma.

Display Painting *California Pastoral*, watercolour and mixed media by Anne Hunter Hamilton.

pages 99–105

Bringing Home the Beach

A poolside pavilion with a vineyard view, this dining and entertaining space overlooks fields planted with grapes, a hillside monastery, and mountains beyond.

Space Sets of sliding, glass-paned doors open the front of the building to the pool and surrounding lawn. To help blur the line between inside and out, the pool house has no thresholds or mouldings around the doors and windows.

Colour Walls and ceilings Fuller O'Brien White Wing, flat, (Benjamin Moore White Heron OC-57).

Furnishings Custom-painted Augusta wicker chairs, Pottery Barn Classic Hotel table linen, blue acrylic plates, glasses, jug, and bowls, Tivoli cutlery, Pottery Barn Classic stemware, block print cushions, Belmont stripe cushion, and ticking stripe cushion, all from Pottery Barn. Grilling accessories from Williams-Sonoma. Contemporary zinc-top table. Antique French enamelware jug from Timeless Treasures Vintage Interiors, San Francisco.

Lighting Outdoor lights with galvanized metal shades. Camp lanterns in grilling area from Pottery Barn.

pages 112–19

Dockside Dining

A beach house overlooking the San Francisco bay is the setting for this inviting wooden jetty, and the ideal spot for swimming, boating, and sunbathing.

Space Steps from the house on a broad sandy beach, the landward end of the dock is provisioned for outdoor grilling, while the water-facing end flares out to provide room for sunbathers and offers a ladder reaching the boat mooring.

Furnishings Tufted cushions, Market umbrella, Espadrille stripe towels and cushions, outdoor occasional table, and acrylic jug, all from Pottery Barn. Adirondack chairs have been given a coat of deck paint for outdoor durability. Vintage basket from The Gardener, Berekeley, California. Wire basket from The Container Store.

pages 122–25

Lighting for Entertaining

This three-storey townhouse hides a small garden patio in the back. The house has classic Victorian details, including ornate mouldings, many fireplaces, and 3.5-m (12-ft) ceilings.

Space Located immediately adjacent to the kitchen, this dining room originally served as the library to the house. The floor-to-ceiling bookshelves and sliding ladders were kept in place when the space was converted to a dining room.

Colour Walls (Benjamin Moore Black Beauty 2128-10, satin).

Furnishings Tufted twill cushions, Hemstich table runner and napkins, Arctic cutlery, and Great Wine decanter, and square decanter, all from Pottery Barn. Reproduction mirrored clock face. Black ceramic bowls and pierced votives from Papaya, Sydney, Australia. Assorted dinnerware from Sue Fisher King, San Francisco.

Lighting Drum shades from Pottery Barn Teen.

Display Flower print from Pottery Barn.

pages 132–37

Storage for an Open-Plan Kitchen

A remarkable view of the ocean can be seen from the top-storey of this shingled cottage. Built in 1884, the house was refurbished in 1998.

Space Custom-designed for ease and organization, the kitchen has Carrara marble worktops and includes a pair of Fisher Paykel dishwashers. In the dining area, built-in storage has drawers and compartments specially sized to fit a variety of tableware and linen.

Colour Walls (Benjamin Moore Pale Celery 2150-60). Trim (Benjamin Moore Snow White OC-66).

Furnishings Megan chairs, Maxime upholstered cube, Sausalito dinnerware in blanca and amber, Cambridge cutlery, Great Wine glasses, Great Wine decanters, Savannah baskets, and Henley rug, all from Pottery Barn. Glazed earthenware bowls from Oliviers & Co, San Francisco. Napkins from Sue Fisher King, San Francisco. Vintage Japanese place mats, wooden trays, and striped linen from Zinc Details, San Francisco.

Lighting Pillar candle ring vintage Pottery Barn.

Display *Flow* series colour prints by Chiaki Misawa courtesy Zinc Details.

pages 148–55

Storage with Style

Originally the town library, this brick structure was built in 1911. Later abandoned and facing demolition, the building was converted to a residence in 1970.

Space The lofty interior of this house is 430 sq m (4,600 sq ft). In the dining room, the original built-in shelves were constructed to hold the library's books. The open-plan interior now houses the homeowners' large collection of art.

Furnishings Megan chairs with linen slipcovers, Pottery Barn white dinnerware, Claro stemware, hammered cutlery, zinc candlesticks, lacquered tray, and Swank barware, all from Pottery Barn. Antique white ironstone, milk glass, and ceramics from Period George, San Francisco. Wool paisley tablecloth from Silk Trading Co., San Francisco. Vintage linen, vintage canisters, silver trophy champagne cooler, and ironwork architectural salvage from Timeless Treasures Vintage Interiors, San Francisco. Linen from The Gardener, Berkeley, California.

Display Charcoal sketches, left to right: Unknown artist. *Seated model*, pencil on paper by Jeppe Vontillius. *Head of a Woman, Clementine, A Farmer's Daughter from Subiaco*, by Franz Johann Heinrich Nadorp.

pages 157–61

Creating a Dining Room Gallery

Built after hillside fires ruined the original home, the current house is a set of interlocking spaces in a strong, contemporary design.

Space The dining room is 4 x 5.5 m (13 x 18 ft), with windows running the length of one side of the room. To the right of the entry, a tiny window among the pictures becomes a framed display.

Colour Walls (Benjamin Moore White Opulence OC-69).

Furnishings Haley table, Gustavian chairs, Great White dinnerware, Great Wine glasses, Luna cutlery, Twist charger and bowl, Monaco vase, wine charms, Bosphorus vases, bookcase, and abaca rug, all from Pottery Barn. Hotel linen napkins from Williams-Sonoma. Architectural salvage, pewter and glass carafe from Paxton Gate, San Francisco. Antique apothecary measures, ironstone platters, and hotel silver from Prize, Berkeley, California. Crystal and silver jugs, from Columbine, Corte Madera, California. Serving utensils and Bento boxes from Swallowtail, San Francisco. Decanters from Zinc Details, San Francisco. Vodka chiller from Tail of the Yak, Berkeley, California.

Display Limited edition etchings by Reesa Tansey.

pages 168–73

A Collector's Kitchen

This 1906 Arts and Crafts cottage was formerly a farmhouse. Extensive plantings surround the house, including a vegetable garden bounded by pleached apple trees.

Space Two small buildings share the property with this large bungalow. Renovated and expanded in the 1970s, the house has scrubbed fir floors and a central kitchen island that was constructed with wood salvaged during the building work.

Furnishings Weathered wooden table, Farmhouse benches, two-tone table linen, Pottery Barn white dinnerware, Arctic cutlery, and solid sisal rug all from Pottery Barn. Verre glasses from Williams-Sonoma. Jugs from Timeless Treasures Vintage Interiors, San Francisco. Glass laboratory jars from Swallowtail, San Francisco. Roseville, Bower, and Owens American art pottery, circa early 1900s, from Naomi's, San Francisco. Contemporary cactus pieces by Arts & Clay Company, Woodstock, NY. Garden green oil jar by Gladdy McBean.

Lighting Warehouse lights.

pages 175–79

Glossary

Acrylic A clear thermoplastic polymer, acrylic is lightweight and impact-resistant, making it perfect for use outdoors. Available in a variety of colours and styles, moulded acrylic tableware can easily accent a casual dinner table.

Adirondack chair During the late nineteenth century, the Adirondack Park holiday spot in northeastern New York state became the inspiration for a style of handcrafted outdoor furniture that uses rough planks from a hemlock tree.

Art pottery These highly collectable, decorative stoneware pieces were produced from the early 1900s to the 1940s, in a range of glazes, patterns, and shapes. Some of the most prolific manufacturers were McCoy, Roseville, and Rookwood – American companies that mass-produced art pottery, which reflected the Art Deco, Art Nouveau, and Prairie Style movements of the period.

Bentwood This style of furniture is made from wood that is bent into shape rather than cut. By soaking or steaming narrow lengths of wood, they can be gently bent into subtle curves. In the mid-nineteenth century, Viennese furniture maker Michael Thonet patented his invention of the bentwood-framed chair that is now a popular seating style in restaurants, cafés, and dining rooms worldwide.

Block print A repeated pattern made on fabric or wallcovering, a block print is transferred to the material's surface through stamping rather than weaving. Typically made from a carved block of hardwood, the stamp can also be made from a linoleum tile or rubber.

Butcher's block This durable surface is made from narrow strips of hardwood, such as maple, oak, cherry, or walnut, laminated together to form a thick cutting board or worktop material. Butcher's block is ideal for kitchen use; it can be maintained with a regular application of mineral oil to keep it from cracking.

Canvas Made from linen or cotton, this heavy-duty fabric is commonly used for sporting goods, awnings, and outdoor furnishings. When used for curtains, loose covers, or cushions, it adds a casual and relaxed feel to a room.

Cedar A natural insect repellent, this aromatic softwood is also resistant to decay. Cedar is often used for building storage chests, linen closets, and outdoor furnishings. Reddish in colour, cedar ages to a beautiful silvery grey over time.

Coin silver This collectable metalware was made from silver coins melted down and reforged. Due to material shortages before the 1859 discovery of the Comstock Lode in Nevada, early American silver was often composed of coin silver, an alloy that is slightly less pure than sterling silver.

Creamware Made of light-coloured clay and fired with an almost colourless glaze, creamware was developed in England in the early 1700s and was, for the next one hundred years, the most widely used pottery in Europe. Wedgwood, who streamlined the classic forms, became its most prolific producer. Printed or painted patterns and borders were sometimes added to the simple shapes of the lightweight earthenware.

Crystal True lead crystal is a type of clear glass that has a percentage of lead oxide (ranging from 24 to 33 percent) that makes it heavier and more brilliant than ordinary glass. The addition of lead also makes crystal softer, easier to cut, and more refractive than glass.

Decanter An ornamental glass vessel designed for holding liquid, a decanter traditionally held wine poured from a bottle. Often made of cut glass, early English and Irish decanters came in a variety of shapes, including square-sided.

Douglas fir Timber from this evergreen tree is a very durable softwood that's commonly used in residential and commercial construction. Interior applications of Douglas fir often include window frames, doors, panelling, ceilings, mouldings, trim, and furniture.

Enamelware Metal dishware coated in thin layers of enamel (a smooth, glassy glaze), enamelware is well suited to use outdoors or in wet areas such as the kitchen, because it's rust-resistant.

Faux suede Designed to mimic the look and feel of genuine napped leather, this durable synthetic is luxurious to the eye and hand. Made of microfibres, it offers a soft, washable upholstery option for dining room chairs.

Gallery Today, a gallery refers to any room or hallway where art collections or photos are displayed. Galleries first appeared (initially without the art) in grand European houses between the sixteenth and eighteenth centuries as long hallways where owners and visitors could exercise during cold or rainy weather. Residents soon began to line these walls with paintings.

Halogen A modern refinement of the incandescent light bulb, these bulbs are filled with halogen gas and offer bright, white light, compact size, energy efficiency, and a longer lifespan than incandescent bulbs. Halogen fixtures cast an illumination that reads truer to natural light than incandescent or fluorescent lighting.

Hotel silver Collected more for its history than for its sheen, hotel silver is generally made of heavy-duty silver plate and often has a stamp or signature of the hotel that commissioned it. Usually in the form of coffee services and tableware, the majority of these pieces date from 1900 to the 1930s, but earlier examples are highly coveted.

Ironstone A durable fired-clay pottery that was developed in England in the nineteenth century, ironstone takes its name from the traces of powdered iron rumoured to be included in its patented formula. Generally thicker than china, ironstone is available in a variety of glazes, colours, and styles.

Jute This strong, woody plant fibre is grown extensively in Asia, and is noted for its natural strength and longevity. When woven, jute has a lush appearance and texture akin to wool. Soft, durable, and stain-resistant, jute rugs are perfect for dining spaces.

Kraft paper This heavyweight paper is made from pulp processed with a sulphur solution. Most frequently used as wrapping paper and for craft projects, kraft paper also makes a great casual table covering. Naturally brown in colour, kraft paper can be found in bleached varieties that are lighter brown or white.

Lazy Susan This type of revolving circular tray was originally intended to sit on a dining table and rotate a selection of relishes, condiments, and the like. These days, a lazy Susan might store a rotating collection of dishware or other household staples within a cupboard.

Linen Woven from the fibres of the flax plant, linen is possibly the first fabric produced by humans. It can be as fine and sheer as a handkerchief or as substantial as a starched napkin. Twice as strong as cotton, linen softens with each washing. This versatile fabric was so commonly used for household textiles, such as tablecloths, napkins, and bed sheets, that the word gained a second definition as the general term for these everyday items.

Mahogany This valuable, close-grained hardwood varies in colour from golden brown to deep red brown, and is used for the manufacture of fine furniture, cupboards, panelling, interior trim, doors, decorative borders, and flooring.

Moulding This architectural detail most commonly refers to the decorative strip of carved wood that finishes doorways, windows, chair rails, ceilings, and walls.

Murano glass An island off the coast of Venice where the most renowned Venetian glass blowers set up their shops, Murano has been the centre of glassmaking since the fifteenth century. Prized for its incredible lightness, transparency, and polychromatic glazes, Murano glass continues to be hand-blown with the traditional techniques.

Oak A durable, richly grained hardwood harvested from an oak tree, this wood is perfect for constructing furniture and flooring. White oak is slightly harder and more rot-resistant than red oak, but both are commonly used in woodworking and are usually finished with a honey stain.

Open plan An open-plan room is designed with few walls or architectural obstructions to create one, large, lofty space. In a dining-kitchen area, the open-plan approach allows creativity with room planning, so that the room can easily serve the purposes of both kitchen and dining room.

Paisley The term "paisley" has become synonymous with the signature tadpole-shaped motif of textiles originally made in India. Typically made of soft wool that has been woven into an intricately patterned shawl, paisley takes its name from the Scottish mill town where these shawls were reproduced. Paisley makes a stylish statement in a dining space.

Panelling Originally used to prevent wall damage from chair backs and heavy-traffic, panelling usually refers to wooden boards that cover the lower portion of a wall. The term can also refer to full-height wall panelling. Beadboard, which has a regular raised pattern on the wood, is a common type of panelling.

Patina When the effects of age and use transform the surface of a material, this is referred to as a patina. A classic example is the green layer that forms on copper or bronze over time when it's exposed to outdoor elements.

Pine One variety of wood that comes from coniferous trees (which produce cones), pine is softer than the types of wood that come from deciduous trees (which shed leaves). Pine is a popular choice for furniture, flooring, and cupboards because of its knotty, rustic grain. Old pine is best for floors. A harder option is white pine, a straight-grained wood with little resin that is often used for interior trim and furnishings.

Polaroid This trademarked name refers to an instantly developed photograph taken with a Polaroid camera. Useful for cataloguing the contents of storage containers, Polaroids can be taped to the outside of a box or kept in a notebook as reference.

Redwood While any wood that produces a red dye is considered a redwood, the most famous are the California coast redwoods, which grow up to 110 m (360 ft) in height. This durable hardwood is used in both interiors and exteriors, including architectural detailing, panelling, decking, and rustic furniture.

Salvaged wood Timber that has been rescued and reused for a new purpose is called salvaged. Often recycled from a refurbishment or complete renovation of an older home, Douglas fir is a common salvaged wood. Redwood and cypress woods are often reclaimed from the bottom of rivers and lakes, where they sank during transport and have since become nearly petrified.

Seagrass Commercially grown in China, seagrass produces a fibre that is similar to straw and smoother than coir or jute. This fibre's durability makes seagrass rugs suitable for high-traffic areas.

Shadow box This shallow, closed-frame box allows you to display and protect three-dimensional artwork, books, or mementos behind glass.

Sideboard A classic piece of dining room furniture with drawers and shelves for linen and tableware, a sideboard usually sits in close proximity to the dining table, so that it can be used as a staging ground for serving dishes.

Silver plate To create a less expensive substitute for solid silver, the process of silver plating was developed in 1743. The initial plating technique involved fusing a sheet of sterling silver to a copper mould, then rolling or hammering the material to create a sandwich of silver over copper. After a century of this technique, which was called Sheffield Plate, a more efficient method of electroplating (or gilding by electrolysis) was developed and eventually became the standard process for the manufacture of tableware and silver-handled cutlery.

Sisal This flexible fibre is made from the leaves of the sisal (or agave) plant, which grows in Africa and South America. Softer to the touch than jute, but still durable, sisal is commonly woven into flat rugs with an even, highly textural surface. Sisal rugs hide dirt, resist stains, and absorb sounds, making them practical for high-traffic areas.

Terracotta Meaning "baked earth", terracotta existed as early as 3000 B.C., when it was used to make pottery vases and statuettes. Its use as an architectural material dates back to ancient Greece, when terracotta roof tiles and decorative elements adorned temples and other structures. Today, tiles made of this natural material are a popular flooring option. Whether glazed, painted, or unglazed, they add warmth and rustic charm to their surroundings.

Voile This lightweight, woven fabric is traditionally made from cotton or silk, but it can also be made of wool or synthetic fibres. Light filters through its sheer weave, so voile curtains make a space feel softly light-infused.

Wicker Created by weaving flexible lengths of plants, such as bamboo, cane, rattan, reed, or willow, around a sturdy frame, wicker is commonly used to make baskets and furniture. A durable material, wicker furniture can stand up to a century of normal use.

Zoning Dividing a room or space into zones or sections reserved for different purposes can be accomplished with the help of furnishings, lighting, or accessories. For example, a dining space might have separate areas sectioned off for a long table, a cosy conversation area, and a staging area for making drinks.

Index

Acknowledgements

Project Editor
Lisa Light

Copy Editor
Peter Cieply

Designers
Adrienne Aquino
Marisa Kwek
Jackie Mancuso

Illustrators
Paul Jamtgaard
Nate Padavick

Indexer
Ken DellaPenta

Photography Assistants
Christian Horan
Bill Moran
David Shinman

Stylist Assistants
Dorsey Blunt
Daniel Dent
Csilla Horvath
Greg Lowe
Julie Maldonado
Lauren Williams

Lead Merchandise Co-ordinator
Tim Lewis

Merchandise Co-ordinators
Peter Jewett
Mark Johnson
Dan Katter
Bryan Kehoe
Peter Martin
Nick McCormack
James Moorehead
Paul Muldrow
Grady Schneider
Mario Serafin
Roger Snell

Weldon Owen thanks the photography and editorial teams for their creativity and stamina in producing this book and acknowledges the following people and organizations for their invaluable contribution in:

Allowing us to photograph their wonderful homes
Howard & Lori Backen, Cindy Brooks & Judith Thompson, Tara Crawford & Chris Frederiksen, Lisa Fuerst, Brian & Jennifer Kelly, Grace Livingston, Dr. Larry & Arlene Klainer, Jim & Kathryn Lino, Karen O'Leary, Jill Poole, Helie Robertson, Rod Rougelot & his canine wonder, Becker, Jessica Seaton & Keith Wilson, Reesa Tansey & Gary Greenfield, Celia Tejada, Bernardo Urquietta, Norma & Robert Wells, and Patrick Wynhoff

Supplying artworks or props
Woody Biggs (Paris Prints), Collage Gallery, Columbine, Tara Crawford & Chris Frederiksen, The Gardener, Thomas Hager, Anne Hunter Hamilton, Laci's, Chiaki Misawa, Nancy Koltes at Home, Naomi's of San Francisco, Nest, Papaya, Paxton Gate, Period George, Prize, Helie Robertson, The Silk Trading Company, Sue Fisher King, Swallowtail, Tail of the Yak, Reesa Tansey, Celia Tejada, Terramoto Ceramics, Timeless Treasures, and Zinc Details

Catering on location
Kass Kapsiak and Peggy Fallon (Catering by Kass), and Andrew Mayne, Arlene Susmilch and Frederick Scott (Stir Catering)

Providing assistance, advice, or support
Allison Arieff, Jim Baldwin, Garrett Burdick, Gregory D. Cann, Val Cipollone, Elizabeth Dougherty, Meghan Hildebrand, Sam Hoffman (New Lab), Anjana Kacker, Kathy Kaiser, Livia McCree, Charlie Path, Ginny Pendleton, Pottery Barn Creative Services, Patrick Printy, Gina Risso, Philip Rossetti, Cynthia Rubin, Anthony Spurlock, Kelly Tagore, Juli Vendzules, Laurie Wertz, and Colin Wheatland

Author Acknowledgement
My Apple iBook, FedEx, and an internet connection made it possible for me to connect with a great group of talented women who worked tirelessly – and with unfailing good humour – for many months on this book. Despite a history-making power failure and several nor'easters, Editor Lisa Light, Managing Editor Sarah Lynch, and Associate Publisher Shawna Mullen were never far when I needed guidance. And right here at home, my husband Stephen, and brand-new baby boy Finn, are always a steadying presence. Thank you.

All photography by David Matheson and styling by Nadine Bush, except for:
Jacket front cover, page 1, photography by Melanie Acevedo and styling by Anthony Albertus. Page 53 (top Material), page 155 (bottom Material), photography by Hotze Eisma. Page 57 (middle Material), page 125 (middle Material), photography by Dan Clark. Page 61 (top right), photography by Stefano Massei and styling by Alistair Turnbull.